NOVA SCOTIA &
THE MARITIMES

BY BIKE ™
21 TOURS GEARED FOR DISCOVERY

NOVA SCOTIA & THE MARITIMES

BY BIKE™
21 TOURS GEARED FOR DISCOVERY

Walter Sienko

THE
MOUNTAINEERS

Published by
The Mountaineers
1001 SW Klickitat Way, Suite 201
Seattle, Washington 98134

9 8 7 6 5
5 4 3 2 1

Published simultaneously in Canada by Douglas & McIntyre, Ltd., 1615 Venables Street, Vancouver, B.C. V5L 2H1

Published simultaneously in Great Britain by Cordee, 3a DeMontfort Street, Leicester, England, LE1 7HD

Manufactured in the United States of America

Edited by Heath Lynn Silberfeld
Maps by Dana Ramsay
All photographs by the author except as noted
Cover design by Watson Graphics
Book layout by Gray Mouse Graphics
Typography by The Mountaineers Books

Cover photographs: *Stanhope Lighthouse on Prince Edward Island National Park.* Inset: *The author near Antigonish*
Frontispiece: *A mill, enshrouded by mist, stands on the banks of the Magaguadavic River, which flows through St. George.*

Library of Congress Cataloging-in-Publication Data
Sienko, Walter.
    Nova Scotia & the Maritimes by bike : 21 tours geared for discovery / Walter Sienko.
        p.   cm.
    Includes index.
    ISBN 0-89886-442-9
    1. Bicycle touring—Nova Scotia—Guidebooks. 2. Bicycle touring—Maritime Provinces—Guidebooks. 3. Bicycle touring—Newfoundland—Guidebooks. 4. Nova Scotia—Guidebooks. 5. Maritime Provinces—Guidebooks. 6. Newfoundland—Guidebooks. I. Title.
GV1046.C22M276   1995
796.6'4'09715—dc20   95–23634
                                                                  CIP

The author passes a moose-crossing sign on the road to Chatham.

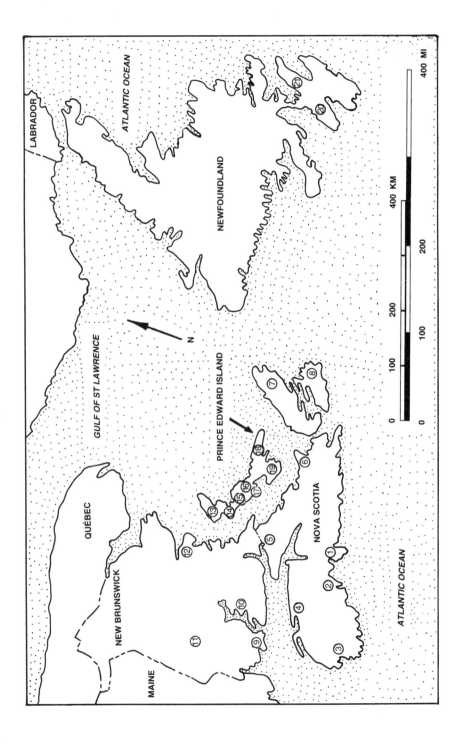

CONTENTS

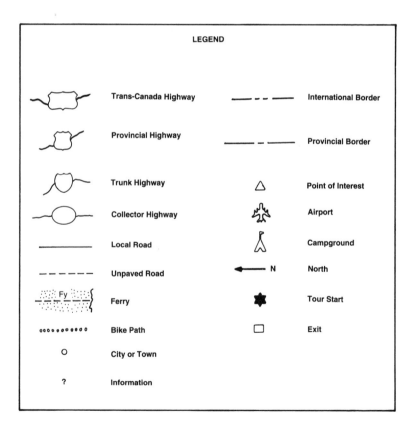

ACKNOWLEDGMENTS

I would like to thank the following for their help: Margaret Foster, editor in chief at The Mountaineers, for encouraging me to write the book; Martin Hollyer and Derek Donn for their fortuitous companionship; the staff at Metropolitan Toronto Reference Library; the exasperated staff at every tourist office I visited; and to everyone who gave me their attention, advice, or just helped me to pass the time during rainy days.

Thanks, Dana, for your patience, encouragement, and love.

PREFACE

This book started as an idea about India. I had finished writing *Latin America by Bike* and I was looking for other adventures and challenges. I approached The Mountaineers, hoping they would think a book on bicycling in India was feasible. They didn't. However, they did ask if I wanted to write a guide to bicycling in Nova Scotia and the Maritimes. I was skeptical. I had never visited this part of my country and it was a grinding of mental gears to move from Varanasi's *ghats* to Newfoundland's outports. But within a couple of weeks I was flying to Halifax, and I never looked back. India is still waiting for me.

I couldn't have imagined how beautiful and rewarding Atlantic Canada (the Maritime Provinces—New Brunswick, Nova Scotia, Prince Edward Island—and Newfoundland) could be. I've cycled in over twenty-five countries, through the Western United States and Alaska, and every Canadian province and territory; I've found that Atlantic Canada offers some of the most peaceful, rewarding riding I've ever done. During my trips in the Maritimes, I rode through sections of magnificent scenery where seeing a car was a rarity. I met people who offered me their homes when the weather looked bleak. I made friends with whales, moose, and crows. I felt the ocean breathe. From my home in Toronto, I had stumbled into an exciting part of my own country that is worth sharing.

Atlantic Canada is perfect for cycling. It doesn't matter if you're a beginner or an expert, you can find a tour for every level. The region has something for everyone; the scenery, people, history, all combine to offer you some of the most rewarding cycling experiences in North America.

You can escape to the wild highlands of Nova Scotia's Cape Breton Island or trundle beside the serene banks of New Brunswick's St. John River. You can follow the stormy seas around Newfoundland's South Shore or trip beside Prince Edward Island's manicured farms. Within this compact region are areas where you can submit to the joys, challenges, and beauty with every pedal stroke.

I often think back to the Maritimers I met during my research: the shopkeepers in Newfoundland who wiled away the day discussing the happenings around town, the artists in Gagetown who enlightened me on Maritime art, the potato farmers on Prince Edward Island who discussed island politics, and the lobster fishing crews who laughed along with my fishing naiveté. Wherever you choose to go in Atlantic Canada, you're going to find openness and a traditional sense of values. I've never felt safer traveling.

I made friends with more than people. In the Maritimes you can still meet moose eye to eye. You can watch deer dance on the roadside. On

Opposite: *A cyclist pedals through the Marram grass and fields in Prince Edward Island National Park.*

the shores and in the waters, seals and whales abound. The wilds of the sea, forest, and air offer some of the best opportunities to see wildlife in North America.

You can also gain a perspective on history that you never knew existed. Atlantic Canada was the fulcrum of power for the struggle for North America. Natives, Acadians—those who settled the French colony of Acadia on the northeast coast of North America, particularly in Nova Scotia and New Brunswick—and waves of immigrants from the United Kingdom and the United States arrived, struggled, and learned to share the land. You become part of history and that history becomes part of you.

If you had to choose a perfect bicycle-touring destination, what more would you look for?

HOW TO USE THIS BOOK

I've divided this book into three sections. The first, General Information, outlines the details you should consider before setting out to tour Atlantic Canada, how to get there, and what you should expect when you arrive. So, if you need information on topics such as what type of clothing to pack, how to get to Atlantic Canada, or whether or not you should camp, look at this section.

The second section, comprising the bulk of the book, I divide into the region's four provinces. Each province description starts with an introduction that gives you a perspective on geography and history. You can also learn about the province's weather and about accommodations. After reading a province description, you should be about ready to begin touring.

Each provincial section contains individual tours that I hope capture its most interesting and alluring areas. Each tour begins with a name and number for quick reference. I've stated each tour's distance in kilometers and miles, but this is the only conversion I make. Because Canada uses the metric system and all signs and directions are in kilometers, that's what I've used in the book. Refer to Appendix 2 for conversion formulas and calibrate your odometer to kilometers. Next, I've given a time estimate. Some tours should only take a day with a normal pace of between 60 and 100 kilometers. Tours that are longer than a day are broken down into daily chunks. I've tried to end each day at a provincial or national park campground. When this wasn't possible, I've ended a day at a town that has plentiful accommodations. If you don't want to camp or the weather is dismal, Appendix 4 lists accommodations available en route. The next bite of information, Terrain, is somewhat subjective. After all, what I consider very hilly may be a blip by your standards, but the descriptor should give you an idea what to expect and how difficult a tour will be.

Under the Maps section, I've listed what I consider to be the best general touring maps available for the tour. All sorts of maps exist, but, ironically, for every province the provincial maps are the best available. They are colorful, have the largest scale, provide the most detail, and, for tourist maps, are accurate. On top of all this, they are free and available at every tourist office or by calling the province's toll-free information line and having the maps sent to you before you go. You could get other maps that depict all of Atlantic Canada, or conversely 1:50,000 topographic maps from the Department of Natural Resources, but this is a bit of overkill. The province's tourist map along with the maps and directions in the book should give you all the information you need.

If you're in Atlantic Canada long enough that you want to do more than one tour, I've added information on the nearest connecting tours. The tours might not literally connect, but the information can help you plan where to go next. The next piece of information is Connections, which tells you about the access routes to a tour. For example, for Tour

No. 1, you'll see that you can access the route via two major highways and an airport. If you're driving and you have a road map, you can determine the best way to get to a tour's starting point. Throughout Atlantic Canada, the federal government supports the construction and maintenance of a national highway system, known as the Trans-Canada Highway and usually numbered as Trans-Canada Highway 1. If the road bisects, it may have designated numbers, such as 102, 103, and so forth, as in Nova Scotia. Each province maintains its own numbering system to designate provincial, trunk, or collector highways. You can refer to the maps to tell one road from another.

Within the introductory section of each tour, I've given a brief description of what to expect and why the tour is special. Sometimes, the scenery is outstanding, while another tour may offer quiet riding, interesting people, and an insight into the area's history or way of life. Each introduction also mentions the availability of supplies, bike shops, and what the general climate and traffic patterns are like.

Each detailed tour description, divided into days if two days or more, guides you through the area, and follows the most interesting and enjoyable routes. Along the way I point out interesting facts or tidbits of history to help you appreciate the area a little more. As you cycle along the Annapolis Valley in Nova Scotia, for example, I hope you can imagine the battles that occurred between the French and British and the tragedy of the Acadians.

Most of the roads in Atlantic Canada are well marked, or at least the signs point to the next town down the road. Still, I list the road numbers and the distances you should travel between landmarks and intersections. You'll find, for example, if you ask a farmer where Route 333 is, he won't know the route's number but will call it "O'Leary Road," after the town the road heads to. Along a route, stop at the tourist offices to see what else is in an area. Fairs and festivals are always taking place and are always worth the time to visit.

The last section of the book is the Appendices. In Appendix 1, I've listed items to take on a bike trip. Obviously this is a general list of things I prefer to take. If you're traveling with someone else, you only need one first-aid kit and one set of tools if the parts match. Feel free to use this as a guide to help you start out, but remember how easy it is to overpack. Appendix 2 includes a metric conversion chart so you won't panic if the weather forecast calls for a high of 18 degrees. Most Maritimers are fairly conservative, and despite Canada officially adopting the metric system over twenty years ago, they still refer to imperial measurements. The temperature chart in Appendix 3 gives you an idea of the temperature ranges of each province and should help you plan when to tour. Appendix 4 is a listing of accommodations for each tour. Appendix 5 provides addresses and toll-free phone numbers for provincial tourist offices.

Well, that's it for these preliminaries. Have fun.

PART I

GENERAL INFORMATION

A cyclist rides past some of the bogs and barrens near Branch, Newfoundland.

DOCUMENTS

Before you leave on a trip to Atlantic Canada you need to prepare documents. First, everyone should carry some form of identification. If you're unfortunate enough to get into an accident or other trouble, proofing your identity is a necessity. Canadians should carry a Health Card and a birth certificate or driver's license. U.S. citizens will need to show proof of citizenship to enter Canada. A passport is ideal, but a birth certificate is usually enough. Individuals under eighteen years of age must either be accompanied by or have written permission from a parent or guardian before entering the country. Citizens from other countries should check document and visa requirements before arriving. Give yourself plenty of time to gather any documents you need. With the minimum of documents, the world's longest unprotected border is one of the easiest in the world to cross.

Consider keeping an extra copy of all documents separate from the originals. The copies will help in case you ever need to replace the originals. I hide the copies in my bike's handlebars and seat post. I also record my bike's serial number and carry a photograph of it. These simple precautions will help you to start your trip securely.

HEALTH

Before you arrive in Atlantic Canada, you should have some type of health insurance. If you are Canadian, a provincial Health Number should cover any expenses. If you are from elsewhere, you can obtain insurance either in your own country or when you arrive in Canada. Some credit card and travelers check companies offer travel insurance plans.

The Maritimes pose no extraordinary health risks. The standard of living and health facilities equal those of the United Sates or Europe. You won't need any special inoculations or shots before traveling, though you might want to get a hepatitis shot in case of an accident. Bring any medication you need, as well as a copy of any prescriptions to prove to Customs you are on medication and in case you need to refill them.

Water poses no health risks; 99.9 percent of the water from taps is safe to drink. There may be rare instances when the groundwater has been contaminated or tastes foul, but in such cases locals will warn you when you ask for water. Potable water is easy to obtain if you ask at stores and restaurants. You shouldn't need a water treatment system, although some travelers carry a water purifier for emergencies. I recommend carrying iodine with you. You can sterilize water by using three drops per liter of water and letting it sit for a half hour. The water may taste foul, but the method is great if you're in a pinch and unsure of the water quality.

Follow the same precautions as you would at home when preparing food. Wash your fruits and vegetables. If you plan to do most of your own cooking your chances of getting an upsetting meal are low. More important are the types of food you eat. Since intense cardiovascular activity burns a tremendous amount of calories, you'll be eating more than you thought you could. Try to maintain a 75 percent balance of carbohydrates in your diet. They're the most efficient foods. Don't be afraid to eat out once in a while, especially since the Maritimes offer exquisite seafood and regional specialties.

See Appendix 1 for a list of items you should carry in a first-aid kit.

MONEY

The Canadian dollar (CDN$) rides a roller coaster against its American counterpart. Although it rises and falls, it has been decades since the Canadian dollar was worth more than the American dollar bill. Just about every Canadian business establishment will accept American dollars, but try to keep a supply of Canadian money since some stores may not know or give you the exact exchange rate. Alternatively, keep some American currency as well, as other proprietors, trying to drum up business, offer specials if you pay in U.S. dollars.

The cost of bicycle touring depends on your preferred style. If you plan to stay at bed and breakfasts (B&B) and eat in restaurants, obviously the cost will be much higher than if you choose to camp in the wild and prepare your meals. Staying in B&Bs is expensive but worth the occasional splurge. Expect to pay from CDN$25 to CDN$50 for a double room. Private campgrounds tend to be priced higher if you travel alone. Food prices are higher than in other places in North America and higher still in Newfoundland and Labrador. Some items, such as bike parts, photographic film, and gasoline, are more expensive in Canada than in the U.S.A.

A shock for visitors buying just about everything in Canada is the additional taxes. Each provincial government charges a Provincial Sales Tax (PST), and the federal government charges a Goods and Services Tax (GST). The total tax for an item could be as high as 18 percent on top of the sticker price. Each province varies the percentage and the items taxed, but the GST (universally despised by Canadians) is charged for most services and goods, excluding food (but including snack food). If you are not from Canada, keep your receipts because you can apply for a rebate of both taxes on purchases of non-consumables. Ask for the appropriate forms at the provincial tourist offices or Customs at the border.

You can access your cash by at least three different methods. The first is cash on hand. Carrying all your cash is risky; if it gets lost, you lose. Travelers checks are the second option. Normally, you have to pay a commission, although if you belong to an automobile club or use certain banks, you might get them for free. Buying the checks in Canadian denominations will make transactions easier. A third convenient method of accessing your money is with a bank card. "Twenty-four-hour tellers" are available in most cities, and for a small fee you can withdraw sums of cash that your bank will deduct from your account at the proper exchange rate. This takes a bit more planning, but if you have travelers checks or a credit card stashed away for emergencies you should have few worries.

Carry your cash, cards, and checks in separate places. I wear a money belt around my waist for my original documents, cash, and credit cards. For my daily cash I use a small waterproof wallet. Don't keep everything in one place, and know how to report and replace any losses.

BICYCLES

You can use any type of bicycle to travel through Atlantic Canada, but the more specialized your bike is for touring the more comfortable your trip will be. Of the four bike species available for your ride, the first is the *Tourus maximus*, the ideal touring machine. Bred with a wide wheel base, ample eyelets for attaching racks and fenders, dropped handlebars with gear shifters at the bar ends, and skinny tires, these bikes are designed for maximum speed and comfortable touring. The second bike species is the *Alpine versatilitus*, or mountain bike. These

A cyclist passes by a few curious cows along the road to Cape St. Mary's.

animals are bred to roam everywhere: over gravel roads, forest trails, and unused railbeds. These bikes are acceptable for touring if you replace the traditional wide, knobby tires with skinny tires and add bar ends to the handlebars so you can adjust hand positions. Sometimes the wider gearing of a mountain bike may be inadequate for keeping a comfortable cadence, so if you find this a nuisance, most bike shops can change the gear ratio easily. Crossbred between the *Tourus maximus* and the *Alpine versatilitus* is the *Utilitus rex*, the hybrid or commuter bike. Originally designed for commuters who wanted more balance from riding in an upright position and with wider wheels, the commuter bike is a compromise for bicycle touring since the gearing ratios are usually insufficient and the components ill designed for the rigors of continuous kilometers. Lower on the evolutionary ladder is the *Tourus desperatus*, the sport/utility bike. Meant to be ridden on Sundays, you can find one of these bikes herded at most department stores or lurking behind the expensive models in bike shops. Certainly, with modifications you could use them to take limited tours, but you could be having more fun with a more evolved bike.

Another option is renting a bike once you arrive. You take your chances though, since shops vary greatly in the types of bikes they offer.

Whatever bike you bring, make sure it fits you properly. When you straddle the bike's top tube, the clearance between your crotch and the top tube should be 2 to 6 centimeters on a touring bike and 8 to 12 centimeters on a mountain bike. Adjust the saddle so that your leg is about 95 percent fully extended at the bottom of your down stroke. A good bike shop will adjust the height and seat tilt and will elevate the handlebars so everything fits properly.

Tools. In certain parts of Atlantic Canada, it can be a long way between bike shops, so you need to prepare for possible calamities. Everyone should know how to repair and replace a bicycle tube. Two of the main causes of flats are underinflated tires and punctures. By keeping your tires properly inflated and in good shape, you can avoid most flats. I replace a flat tube and repair it in the evening. Other tools you should carry include allen wrenches to fit all the bolts on your bike and a 6-inch crescent wrench. You want to be able to adjust your gears, brakes, handlebars, and cables. I try not to mess with the headset, pedals, and wheel bearings on the road unless it is an emergency. If bearings start creaking, I can usually ride to the nearest bike shop before any damage occurs. If you are confident about your repair knowledge, carry a spoke wrench, chain breaker, freewheel remover, and cone wrenches. If you don't know how to use these tools, do not bother to bring them along. Finally, if there is any chance you might have to ride through rain, bring chain oil.

While touring, check your equipment periodically. Make sure you keep the tires well inflated, the wheels true, the brakes and headset well adjusted, and the racks secure.

Accessories. While riding, you need certain extras to make your trip more comfortable and safe. First, you need racks to carry your gear. Technically, you should carry 60 percent of your gear on a rear rack and 40 percent on the front rack. If you carry a minimum of gear, a rear rack and a handlebar bag should suffice. Try to use a rear rack that attaches to both seat stays. The best design for a front rack is one that centers the bags at the wheel's hub. This allows for more control but needs more hardware to install. Buy the strongest, safest racks you can; trust me, you don't want to be rocketing down the 12-percent grade of French Mountain in Cape Breton and have a cheap rack snap into your wheel.

You also need some bags in which to carry your gear. Bike bags, called panniers, attach to the racks with a combination of straps and hooks. Use the most durable, waterproof, and secure bags you can. When you fit them on your bike, make sure your heels have enough clearance so they don't hit the bags when you pedal. Don't try to carry your gear in a backpack; not only is this ultimately damaging to the nerves in your wrists and neck, it's also dangerously unbalanced and interferes with your rear view.

Bring an odometer with you to take the guesswork out of how much farther you have to go. It doesn't have to be complex or expensive.

A bell is a necessity. In some provinces it is illegal to ride without one. I find them useful as a warning to others that I'm coming. Despite the plethora of horns, whistles, and alarms available for bikes, I still love the instant recognition of a tinkling bike bell.

Although most Maritimers are honest, alas, evil still lurks in large cities, and the most evil are bike thieves. Preferably, bring a cable lock that can secure both wheels. In cities always lock your bike, and outside cities, if you have to leave your bike for more than a few minutes, lock it.

CLOTHING

A helmet should always be sitting snugly on top of your head. When you're cycling along a rustic, lonely road on Prince Edward Island (PEI) it might seem silly to be sweating under a helmet. Yet, despite the dreariness of carrying and donning a helmet, it may save your life. Wearing a helmet should become so habitual that when you're not using it you feel unsafe. PEI and New Brunswick are planning to pass laws making bicycle helmets mandatory, and the city of St. John's, Newfoundland, has already passed a municipal law to this effect.

I like wearing a cycling jersey. Designed for comfort and practicality, the best are made from a material that is easily washable. If you don't want to look like a pretentious cyclist, you could just as easily wear a T-shirt. Instead of carrying a sweater or long-sleeved shirt, I carry a pair of arm warmers.

You will need a jacket for warmth and to use as a windbreak. You'll be glad you have a good jacket on cold, windy mornings. The best are designed for cycling: cut low in the back, long in the arms, and brightly colored for visibility. I have yet to find a material that is really waterproof. Most materials that claim breathability and waterproofing capabilities break down after long exposure and won't breathe if they are dirty. But if you feel such jackets are worth the price, try one.

One of the most important pieces of clothing you need to consider is your cycling shorts. When your day includes six hours of cycling, a good pair of shorts is invaluable. Full racing shorts, in customary black, are ideal if the chamois (padding) is made of an easily washable material. A natural chamois needs meticulous care. Touring shorts have a terrycloth chamois and are made of cotton. Do not ride with a pair of jeans or gym shorts; if you do, painful chafing and rubbing will occur quickly.

Whatever shoes you decide to take with you, they should have stiff soles and be durable. Ideally, use cycling shoes without cleats or cycling shoes with a recessed cleat. If you don't want cycling shoes, a good compromise is a pair of lightweight walking shoes because they allow you to walk comfortable distances. Running shoes cause foot fatigue and will wear out quickly. Bring at least two pairs of light cotton socks so you can alternate washings. If you plan to hike, bring a thicker pair of socks to minimize blistering.

I also carry a pair of cycling gloves, which have a variety of uses. They reduce the pressure on your palms, you can brush debris off your tires, and they protect your hands during an accident.

For the times that you are not cycling, your casual clothes should be compact, light, and easy to clean. I usually bring one pair of nylon pants, a T-shirt, shorts that double as swimming trunks, two pairs of underwear, and a pair of light wool gloves.

Sunglasses are a necessity. They offer protection from ultraviolet rays, bugs, dust, and rain. Bring a good pair that feels light, comfortable, and will not slide off your nose when you start sweating.

WEATHER

If you want to avoid cold, wet weather, you can't start cycling any earlier than late April, and even then you could experience it. Except in Newfoundland, May is a good month to start; flowers are in bloom and the tourist rush is a couple of months away. June is even better and is a good time to start in Newfoundland; the days are long enough that you can be cycling until 9:00 in the evening. The tourists will start trickling into the area in June, however, and the blackflies and mosquitoes could be annoying. By this time, the wind and rain should have tapered off. In July and August, the weather is perfect for cycling: the winds have died down, the temperatures are warm enough, the rain is sporadic, and by the middle of August, most of the mosquitoes have disappeared, although they will be replaced by tourists.

Summer is a busy time for tourism in the Maritimes. Accommodations fill up quickly, the main tourist roads can be crowded, and you will be another tourist face in the crowd. The crowds begin to dissipate by the first weekend in September (Labour Day). The weather is still warm enough for cycling, but farther north in Cape Breton and Newfoundland you could find snow. The scenery becomes dramatic as the maple and birch leaves change colors. However, the wind and rain increase in September. Just keep in mind that every season has its advantages and disadvantages. Pick your most convenient time and pack for your trip.

TRANSPORTATION

No matter what methods of transportation you use to arrive in Atlantic Canada you have to negotiate carrying your bike. Airlines may request any number of variations of how they want your bike packed. As a guideline, domestic flights from the United States charge a flat rate for bikes and you must box them. Canadian domestic airlines require that you turn the handlebars, remove the pedals, deflate the tires, and remove any loose items, such as water bottles and odometer. If your bike is one of your two pieces of allocated baggage, it goes free. Before buying your ticket, check with your airline and adhere to its policies. Each province has an international airport, but anyone can fly to a city close to the border and take a train or bus from there.

Trains are the easiest way to transport a bike in Canada, but government policies are closing down and ripping up rail services in the Maritimes. Each year more trunk lines are shut down. Still, the main line through New Brunswick and Nova Scotia schedules at least one train per day. Depending on the station, you could just hand the bike

Grand Manan V, the ferry to Grand Manan Island, is docked at North Harbour.

to a baggage attendant. Trains without baggage cars may not take your bike immediately so you might have to wait at your destination until it arrives.

Buses are fastidious about shipping bikes. Check with the company beforehand. Most long-distance and interprovincial companies require that you box your bike (you have to supply the box) and charge you by weight. Within a province, buses may take your bike, if there is room. Your best chances lie in taking the first bus of the morning or the last bus of the day. It can be difficult to travel by bus during the peak tourist season.

Many bicycle tourists prefer to load their bikes onto their cars, drive to a tour's starting point, ride the tour, and then take their cars to a new area. If you don't have a van or station wagon, you will need a bike carrier. When you pick a carrier, make sure it will fit your bike and the number of bikes you want to carry. Bumper-mounted models may hold one or two bikes, but trunk and top carriers can hold up to four. When you load your bike, take off any loose items and make sure any contact points between the bike and carrier are protected. On trunk-mounted carriers make sure the bike isn't touching the exhaust pipe and the bike's wheels are not so low that they will hit the ground when you hit a bump, and be careful parking.

An extensive ferry system operates throughout Atlantic Canada; some ferries simply cross rivers, others are week-long trips. Generally, the smaller and more frequent the ferry, the easier it is to travel. For example, the ferry system connecting the banks of the St. John River in New Brunswick is free and you may have to summon it from the opposite bank with a buzzer. The ferry between North Sydney, Nova Scotia, and Argentia, Newfoundland, requires at least a 2-day reservation if you don't have a car. If ferries charge, they usually charge a flat rate for bikes that you pay when you board. Check with companies for the schedules, reservations, and prices as they change yearly. Any of the province's toll-free information lines will provide the information (See Appendix 5).

ACCOMMODATIONS

When cycling in the Maritimes, you will most likely use both indoor lodging and camping. If you want to use indoor lodging exclusively, you limit yourself to certain tours. If you choose to pay for indoor accommodations or for camping in the peak season, you need to reserve as far ahead as possible, particularly during the high season or on festival weekends.

Indoor Lodging. The bicycle tourist can use three types of lodging. Hotels are the most expensive and impersonal. They usually offer parking, an outdoor pool, and a restaurant. Bring your bike into your room with you. The larger your group the less expensive the room— hotels are ridiculously expensive if you travel alone. But regardless of the cost, if the weather is terrible and the day's riding has been especially grueling, you may want to splurge for a room.

Bed and Breakfasts. B&Bs have become a way of life for tourists traveling by car. Usually, they're operated by a family that has extra bedrooms for travelers to rent. You might be a little unnerved about arriving and staying in someone's home, but the family atmosphere and congeniality of most B&B operators will make you feel comfortable quickly. The breakfast part of the B&B experience varies with each establishment. Some offer all-you-can-eat meals while others may set out some muffins and orange juice. Ideally, a good B&B offers comfort and a place to meet other travelers. The problem with the good ones is that during the tourist season they fill up as quickly as your panniers before a trip. Sometimes, finding a room is easier if there are two or more in your party; some operators are reluctant to rent a room at a single price because they can make more money by charging for a double or triple room. All the provinces have a toll-free reservation system—use it. Most B&Bs also provide a safe area where you can lock your bike.

Youth Hostels. Some bicycle tourists love them; others hate them. They can be a great place to meet other cyclists and travelers from around the world. They provide a safe place to keep your bike, and unlike other types of accommodations, most have kitchen facilities you can use.

I avoid youth hostels. I find the dormitory rooms confining and filled with travelers more intent on staying up late and unintentionally disturbing others. The only use I have for such accommodations is in large cities where the price for a single bed is noticeably lower than at a B&B. Prepare for late-night interruptions by bringing ear plugs and a sleeping mask.

Camping. For me, the greatest benefit of bicycle touring is the independence of the road—the opportunity to feel the elements and to surround yourself in, well, your surroundings. For me, camping is an inherent part of bicycle touring. Seeing more stars in the sky than you ever thought possible and hearing the ocean waves whisper their lullabies are sublime moments.

When you pay for camping, the costs and facilities vary tremendously. In the national and provincial park systems you cannot book ahead; you try to grab the best spot you can. If you arrive late in the evening, you may camp next to a primitive latrine. Campground services differ; some may not have running water while others offer fire pits and firewood. If you stay in private campgrounds, listed by the tourist offices or not, expect most to have hot showers and adequate facilities. Some campgrounds offer separate non-serviced sites that provide more protection and solitude than the sites serviced for every option imaginable. Private campgrounds can get expensive if you travel on your own as most charge per site rather than per person. You can always try to bargain, claiming you are on your bike, you are alone, or it is not the tourist season.

Free Camping. What if you felt paying for a piece of ground to sleep on wasn't worth it and you chose to sleep as cheaply and quietly as you could? You would have to rely on your ingenuity, spirit, and a smattering of luck. You can do it easily and probably have the best experiences of your trip. People love meeting travelers and bike tourists.

Generally, crown (public) lands require that you obtain permission from the government before you can legally pitch your tent for the night. So your best bet is to ask landowners for permission to camp on their land. I rarely have been refused permission, and I have been on the receiving end of some great experiences because I went out of my way to meet people and spend time with them. When you have received the go-ahead from the owner, or whoever can give you permission, where will you pitch your tent? Your site should be free of protruding rocks and tree stumps and provide good drainage. Don't camp in low-lying, dried-up swamp or below the low-tide mark on beaches. Watch for overhanging branches or rocks because if you have to get up in the middle of the night to answer nature's call, you could get more than you expected. Always leave your site in the condition you found it; whatever you bring in, haul out. How you treat the land reflects on all the bicycle tourists who will come after you. I've spent over five years on the road cycling, a majority of it free camping. If you're sensible, polite, and anticipate possibilities, you shouldn't run into problems. I never have.

When you choose your camping equipment, it's always tempting to buy equipment you can't afford. Give in. Bicycle camping is rigorous, and the better your equipment the more you will enjoy the experience. Who needs to wake up in a tent that has turned into a wading pool or a ruined sleeping bag that has sucked every bit of warmth from your body? Mix the right formula of weight, compactness, versatility, and durability in all your equipment.

Starting with your tent, do not carry one larger than you need. Look for a combination of weight, ease of setup, and resistance to water. Sleeping bags come in three types: the rectangular, offering more cold spots than a refrigerator; the semi-mummy, which tapers toward the feet (warmer than the rectangular but more confining); and the aptly named mummy bag, confining but most heat efficient. Sleeping bags use one of two insulators: down, which is light and compact, is difficult to care for and will not insulate you if it gets wet, and synthetic fills, which are heavier and bulkier but will insulate you if they get wet. Whatever bag you choose, try to get one rated to -10 degrees Celsius if you plan to camp in spring or fall. If it does get colder than your bag rating, you can always wear extra clothes. The second most important insulator is a good sleeping pad, one that comforts your body from the concrete-like ground at campsites and the rocks and tree roots you failed to see when you set up your tent. Although you could use the cheaper foam pads, a self-inflating model is light, compact, and extremely efficient.

The truly independent bicycle tourist will bring a cooking stove. The most important factor in choosing one is the type of fuel it uses. In most of Atlantic Canada you can find camping fuel and white gas at hardware stores and outdoor stores. The problem is that sometimes you'll find it only in four-liter cans. The blue propane gas cartridges are difficult to find outside the main cities, and kerosene is very difficult to find. If you want to cook, remember to bring a pot and a lid, a spoon, potholder, utility knife, and pot scrubber, along with all the kitchen gadgets you want (remember the corkscrew).

FOOD AND DRINK

Eating as much as you want is one of the joys of bicycle touring, but use common sense about what you eat. Breakfasts should be filling, healthy, and not greasy. The "Lumberjack's Special" of fried eggs, sausage, fries, and steak will slow you down. Fat takes far more oxygen and water to burn than carbohydrates. Instead of a formal lunch, snack on high-energy foods like granola, bread, and fruit. During supper, fill up on easy-to-digest foods, such as pasta and rice, that will help your body refuel for the next day. Cycle tourists should try to eat about 75 percent carbohydrates in their diet, mostly grains, fruits, and vegetables.

Like elsewhere in North America, you can buy costly, insubstantial food (usually greasy and inadequate) at average restaurants. On more isolated tours you will have little choice of restaurants—you eat wherever and whatever you can. The bigger the town, the better the variety of food you'll find. Some small villages, particularly on Prince Edward Island, may not have any food stores or restaurants. Learn to be creative when your food supplies are dwindling. Try to stock at least a meal ahead and pick up snacks as you find them.

Finding potable water should not be a problem. You can ask for water at restaurants, stores, gas stations, and nearby houses. In some parts of Newfoundland and in the interior of New Brunswick, you need to be able to carry a full day's water supply.

Drink before you start feeling thirsty; on hot days, you can dehydrate easily. Most tap water is potable, but there are rare cases when a district's groundwater may be contaminated and you will have to rely on bottled water. Unless you plan to bicycle off road for long periods of time, there's no need to carry a water purifier. If you plan to camp in the wild, you should have a method of carrying enough water for your evening's needs (at least three to four liters per person).

TRAFFIC

City traffic seems to be the same everywhere: frenzied people intent on driving as quickly and selfishly as possible. Always be careful when you ride through cities. The worst scenarios are cars turning in front of you, grates, and potholes. Keep your ears and eyes open. Outside of cities, traffic is more controlled and calmer. The tours in this book avoid the main highways unless necessary; instead, they follow secondary roads where most of the traffic is non-commercial. Watch for tourists in newly rented motorhomes. They're probably unaccustomed to maneuvering their big rigs and are ignorant of the draft they create when they pass a cyclist. A rearview mirror is a good investment. If you notice a dangerous circumstance developing, be prepared to move onto the shoulder. Other miscellaneous hazards to keep alert for are train tracks (cross at right angles), merges and turnoffs (be visible, signal, and be predictable), parked cars (use your peripheral vision to see if the driver is in the car), wet roads (slow down on turns and be aware that the painted lines are more slippery), and dogs (if the situation seems dangerous and the dog hasn't stopped at the edge of its territory, you can stop and keep your bike between the two of you).

Visibility is a major factor in traffic safety. The easier it is for a driver to see you, the more predictable you both become. You can use flags, safety vests, or brightly colored clothes so that drivers can recognize and react to you. Avoid riding at night and be especially careful riding into the sun and rain. Carry a red blinking light to use on rainy and foggy days.

In all the Atlantic provinces, cyclists must obey the same traffic laws as motorists, including stopping at traffic lights and stop signs and signaling lane changes and turns. You should ride in a single file and as far to the right as possible. If you have to stop, move off the road.

A final tip: Become accustomed to your loaded bike's handling. Riding an unloaded machine is far different from riding one loaded down with 15 kilograms of gear.

A NOTE ABOUT SAFETY

Safety is an important concern in all outdoor activities. No guidebook can alert you to every hazard or anticipate the limitations of every reader. Therefore, the descriptions of roads, trails, routes, and natural features in this book are not representations that a particular place or excursion will be safe for your party. When you follow any of the routes described in this book, you assume responsibility for your own safety. Under normal conditions, such excursions require the usual attention to traffic, road and trail conditions, weather, terrain, the capabilities of your party, and other factors. Keeping informed on current conditions and exercising common sense are the keys to a safe, enjoyable outing.

The Mountaineers

PART II

21 TOURS GEARED FOR DISCOVERY

Pilot whales, frolicking in groups, display their tails and fins in the waters around Cape Breton Island.

NOVA SCOTIA

INTRODUCTION

Geography

If you use your imagination, Nova Scotia looks like a lobster. The mainland is its body and tail; Cape Breton is the crushing claw. The cyclist can divide the province into three main regions: the rugged coastline dotted with fishing villages, the rolling fertile interior of farms and forest, and the highlands that sweep from Amherst up to the tip of Cape Breton and then plummet into the Atlantic Ocean. The main bodies of water in the Maritimes—the Atlantic Ocean, the Gulf of St. Lawrence, the Bay of Fundy, and the Northumberland Strait—almost turn the province into an island and create 7,400 kilometers of coastline. No point of Nova Scotia sits more than 56 kilometers from the sea.

History

The Micmac were the first people to call Nova Scotia home. Archaeological evidence shows that early Asians crossed the frozen land mass called Beringia that linked Alaska and Siberia sometime during the last Ice Age, which occurred 150,000 to 12,000 years ago. The Micmac, part of the Algonquin linguistic group, were a hunting, fishing, and gathering group that lived in the interior as family groups during the winter. After the spring thaws, the clans would gather to fish and farm, preparing for the following winter. At the time of the first European contact the Micmac population was about 1,000. Today, small communities of Micmacs live on Cape Breton Island, valiantly trying to hold onto the remnants of their culture despite the barrage of tourists and technology.

Some historians believe that the Vikings were the first Europeans in Nova Scotia, but except for a runic stone (now in the Yarmouth Museum) little proof exists of Norse settlements. More likely, Portuguese fishing crews, relentless in their search for cod and whales, traveled to the teeming Grand Banks in the 1400s. In 1497 John Cabot was the first European explorer to land in Cape Breton, but it wasn't until 1605, over 100 years later, that Samuel de Champlain founded the first permanent settlement north of Florida at Port Royal near today's Annapolis Royal. In 1621, Great Britain's monarch, strengthening his hold on the New Dominion, made Nova Scotia the New World's first colony. To prime English emigration, Sir William Alexander, a Scotsman empowered by King Charles I to colonize the territory, promised new settlers 40 hectares of free land. The British

Lake O'Law and two of the Three Sisters Mountains

subjects who arrived were mentally and physically unprepared for the back-breaking job of clearing the virgin forest. Subsequently, British immigration remained only a trickle.

French settlers from Normandy and Brittany were more successful than the English. With the help of master dike builders, the French began cultivating reclaimed land, now fertile with silt, along the shore. This success threatened the British. In 1755, English authorities expelled the Acadians, claiming they were undesirable subjects. New England Planters, who helped deport the Acadians, then snatched the valuable farm land. After the Treaty of Utrecht the Acadian exiles trickled back to their land but found it irrevocably occupied. Today the Acadian culture still thrives along the French Shore, the Pubnicos, and pockets of Cape Breton Island.

Nova Scotia was the stage for dramatic battles between the super-powers of France and Britain. The French, reinforced by the Fortress of Louisbourg, controlled the mouth of the St. Lawrence River—tactically important as the gateway to the interior. The English, to counterbalance the French advantage, built the military complex of Halifax. After sieges and raids, Louisbourg finally fell to the English in 1759. Today, the reconstructed fort is one of North America's most impressive histori-cal attractions.

After the superpowers settled their differences and Britain con-trolled the area, other groups began to immigrate. The Scots and Irish were the major nationalities to arrive, but German Protestants, excelling at fishing and boat building, settled around Lunenburg. Their craftsmanship culminated in the *Bluenose*, the famous racing and fishing schooner, now depicted on the back of the Canadian ten-cent piece. The Great Potato Famine of the eighteenth century forced the immigration of starving Irish by the thousands. Another mass mi-gration occurred during the American Revolution when 25,000 United Empire Loyalists—some of the most educated and cultured people of the time—moved to "New Scotland" rather than becoming citizens of the United States Republic. African-Americans, via the Underground Railway, also hoped to find refuge in Nova Scotia. Until the 1960s, Halifax was home to Canada's largest concentration of Afro-Americans. The last influential migration came in the nineteenth century, when many Scots, forced by famine and oppression to leave their Scottish Highlands, settled in Cape Breton, New Glasgow, and Antigonish. Today, Gaelic people celebrate their heritage with festivals, gatherings of the clans, and studies at Gaelic College on Cape Breton Island.

Weather

Realistically, you could start cycling as early as the end of April and as late as mid-October in southern Nova Scotia. As you move northward to Cape Breton the cycling season shortens. You could be slogging through snow flurries if you ride in Cape Breton in mid-April and mid-October. Nova Scotia's most predictable period for enjoyable cycling is from the middle of May to about the end of September. During these shoulder months, nights may become frosty. Average summer temperatures range between 20 degrees Celsius during the day and 10 degrees at night.

Rain can fall at any time during the cycling season, but spring and autumn receive the most precipitation. Be aware of storm warnings; strong winds and torrential rain can make camping intolerable and cycling dangerous. The wind, strong most of the year, peaks in spring and fall. Because of the area's various weather influences, rely only on the next day's weather forecast, and even then believe it with a pinch of skepticism. I've listened to current weather reports that were the exact opposite of what was really happening.

Nova Scotia's tourism doesn't shift into high gear until July and August. Outside these busy times, tourist sites, campgrounds, and lodging may be closed.

Accommodations

If you plan on using bed and breakfasts and hotels, you can use Nova Scotia Tourism's Check-In Service (the same phone number as the tourism information number in Appendix 5). By calling a toll-free phone number, you can make advance reservations for any government-licensed rooms. make reservations if you can; during high season rooms can be hard to find. If you can't use the reservation system, arrive at your destination early and use the local tourist bureau to help you find a place to stay. Every tourist office will have a listing of accommodations throughout the province.

The private campgrounds, registered and inspected by the government, are also on the reservation and listing service. As you cycle along you'll pass informal private campgrounds, advertised locally and operated independent of licensing. Camping is relatively expensive compared to the value of a good B&B, but you can try to negotiate the standard camping rates. Provincial and national parks operate campgrounds from June to early September. Camping fees are reasonable and standard, regardless of the services each provides. You can't reserve ahead at government campgrounds; whoever arrives first, gets a site.

Free camping is fairly easy, but ask permission from the landowner or a nearby resident. Few people have a problem when free camping, as long as you're discreet, limit your stay to the night, and don't leave a mess.

TOUR NO. 1

PEGGYS COVE

Start / Finish: Halifax (Armdale Rotary)
Distance: 94 kilometers (56.5 miles)
Estimated time: Normally 1 day; 2 days with an overnight
Terrain: Flat to slightly rolling
Map: Nova Scotia—The Doer's and Dreamer's Complete Map
Connecting tours: Tour No. 2
Connections: Highways 102 and 103, Halifax International Airport

If you have just arrived in Nova Scotia by way of the Halifax airport, this tour will prime your excitement for later adventures. If you have arrived from other parts of the province, Peggys Cove is worth seeing for the post-glacial landscape. This short tour typifies the province: pine forests hugging the road, unspoiled fishing villages slumbering by the sea, and, of course, attracting visitors from around the world, Peggys Cove.

Pick up supplies in Halifax before you leave. The restaurant at Peggys Cove and other supplies en route tend to be expensive. Also, try to avoid the intense commuter traffic on weekdays between 7:30 and 9:00 in the morning and between 4:30 and 6:00 in the afternoon. The heaviest traffic flows between Whites Lake and Halifax. During the summer months, daily tour buses march along the road like methodical ants between their hill and a honey spill.

The weather can change quickly. Halifax may be warm and sunny while Peggys Cove experiences drizzling rain. Swirling winds may blow around St. Margarets Bay.

Halifax (Armdale Rotary)/Halifax (Armdale Rotary): 94 kilometers

Begin the tour at the **Armdale Rotary**. If you are inexperienced with traffic circles, use extra care and walk your bike to the correct exit. Follow the signs for **Highway 3**, also named **Bay**, short **for St. Margarets Bay Road**. The longest climb of the day begins as you leave the rotary. Drivers are usually polite and there is a paved, albeit rough, shoulder. The most grueling part of the climb is the first 1.5 km. Cross the **overpass** for Highway 102 and continue straight past the lights at the following intersection. About 2.3 km beyond this intersection is the turn

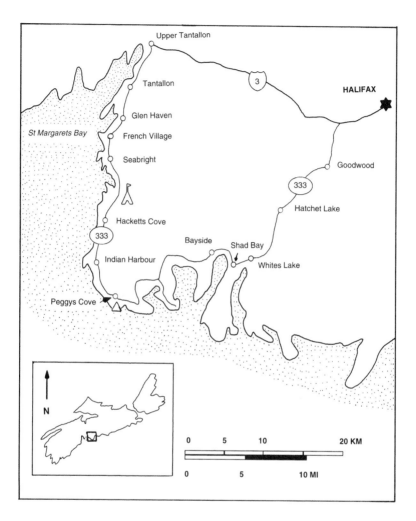

for **Highway 333** to **Peggys Cove**. Carefully, turn left. As you cycle along this road, the smell of pine replaces the smells of the city. Quickly, the business development succumbs to the forest. Over the next 16 km you pass the villages of Goodwood, Hatchet Lake, and Whites Lake. At Whites Lake is the turn for Terence Bay and Lower Prospect; both villages, despite their proximity to Halifax, have remained alluring.

Continuing on **Highway 333**, after 1 km you reach a left turn to Prospect, another fishing village facing the open Atlantic, 12 km down the road. Staying on the main road, you climb over a small headland to reach **Shad Bay**. Beyond this village, you begin skirting small coves. Blue fishing boats, moored to small homemade docks, bob in the inky

The bas-relief monument carved by William deGarthe outside the village of Peggys Cove

water. Fishermen's cottages nestle in the verdant forest. Passing **Bayside**, after another 11 km you reach the junction for McGraths Cove and East Dover. The scenery shifts dramatically.

The geological area around Peggys Cove is known as the Pennant Barrens. The first things you notice are slabs of granite bedrock and dwarf trees, stunted by the poor sediment and salt spray. Glaciers from the last Ice Age, 12,000 years ago, left their debris—these scattered boulders known as erratics.

After about 9 km, watching for cormorants and herons in the bogs, you arrive at the turn for **Peggys Cove**. A short 0.5 km to your **left** and you arrive at the government parking lot on the outskirts of the village. You can leave your bike safely by the attendant's post as you explore on foot.

The salty tang of the sea fills the air. Gulls may be screeching over a discarded cod head. Perched on the worn, tan bedrock, scraped clean by glaciers and sterilized by the salt spray, are the bright white lighthouse, a restaurant and gift shop, and the small cottages of fishermen's families. Red and white trawlers dip and bob in the small sheltered harbor. Peggys Cove looks like the quintessential fishing village. The human element and the austere natural surroundings make it an ideal spot for meditation and exploration. Be careful on the rocks, though: signs warn visitors that "swells and breaking waves may unexpectedly rise over the rocks even on fine and calm days. . . .Visitors have lost their lives in the past."

Once the haunt of poets, painters, and photographers, Peggys Cove has become a victim of its success. A motorcoach association estimates more than 3,000 tour buses visit yearly and this small, once unassuming village is the third most visited tourist spot in Canada. Yet its popularity isn't surprising. Everyone needs a time to remember the force and dignity of nature. The cove's stark landscape of barren bedrock and ever-changing sea gives each of us that time. Maybe you'll be seduced by the sensuous rhythm of the sea as the swells caress the precipices. Or maybe you'll be overwhelmed by the slamming power of the waves as they explode against the rocks. Peggys Cove manifests many moods.

Before leaving, you should stop at the small park across from the parking lot. This small enclosure displays the late William DeGrathe's monument to the inshore fishery. From a 30-meter granite outcropping, Mr. DeGrathe carved a sculpture depicting a guardian angel overlooking thirty-two fishermen and their families, including "Peggy of the Cove," a lone survivor of a nearby shipwreck.

When you leave Peggys Cove, return to **Highway 333** and continue **left** toward Tantallon. As you cycle up the slight hill, gaze back on the village. Now, its small lighthouse and restaurant stand sentinel over the small human settlement surrounded by sky, sea, and rock. As the road begins sliding inland, the landscape, strewn with boulders and outcroppings, switches to fir and spruce forest. After 8 km, the road begins to level out and you pass **Indian Harbour**. For another 18 km, following the shore of St. Margarets Bay, you pass the villages of **Hacketts Cove**, **Seabright**, **French Village**, **Glen Haven**, and **Tantallon**. Another 26 km past Peggys Cove takes you to the end of 333 at **Upper Tantallon**. Turn **right** toward **Halifax** on **Highway 3**. If you were to turn left, you would connect with Tour No. 2. You will arrive at the **Armdale Rotary** in 24 km. As you whiz back downhill to the rotary, be alert for cars.

TOUR NO. 2

BLUENOSE COUNTRY

Start/Finish: Halifax/Liverpool
Distance: 216.1 kilometers (130 miles)
Estimated time: 3 days
Terrain: Flat to slightly hilly
Map: Nova Scotia—The Doer's and
Dreamer's Complete Map
Connecting tours: Tour Nos. 1 and 3
Connections: Highways 102 and 103

Deep history and sparkling oceans fill this tour. The first and longest day's cycling curves past bright beaches, beside coves peppered with islands, and around peninsulas dotted with fishing hamlets. The second day passes Mahone Bay and its mysterious islands, and you finish the day at Lunenburg, Nova Scotia's most beautiful town. The tour's last day is the most isolated as you cycle along wide-open sea and dense forests.

You could add Tour No. 1 to the tour's beginning and Tour No. 3 at the tour's end. If you are worried about time or distance, you could avoid the Aspotogan Peninsula and ride to Bridgewater between East LaHave and LaHave. The traffic along this tour is low to moderate; the only intense traffic is around Halifax. You will find bike shops at Halifax and at Blue Rocks near Lunenburg, but general provisions are easy to obtain except for the stretch between LaHave and Liverpool. Be prepared for occasional fog and rain.

Halifax to Graves Island Provincial Park: 96 kilometers

The tour begins at the **Armdale Rotary**. Following **Highway 3**, climb the 1.5-km hill to the **overpass** of 103. About 2.3 km farther you come to the intersection with Highway 333 to Peggys Cove. Continue straight unless you choose to add the tour for Peggys Cove. After 13 km, you cross 103 and continue on 3. The section between Halifax and Upper Tantallon is the most monotonous of the trip, but ah, how the smell of pine fills your senses. Continue cycling for another 8 km to Upper Tantallon. Shortly beyond this small hamlet, you reach St. Margarets Bay. The road follows a slightly hilly and lightly populated area. Beyond Upper Tantallon 2 km, you pass **Head of St. Margarets Bay**. After another 5.5 km you pass **Boutiliers Point**, where you can enjoy the

A schooner and trawler, two of the Fisheries Museum of the Atlantic's ships, are moored at the Lunenburg dock.

views of jaunty sailboats, charming cottages, and small islands posing in the bays.

The islands you see throughout this tour are drumlins, land masses caused by glacial drift from the last Ice Age. Throughout history various people have used these islands. They were used by the Micmacs for fishing outposts, by privateers for caching treasure, and by rum runners for eluding the coast guard. Today, the bays offer a refuge for wildlife. Sheltered by the climatic influences of the Atlantic Ocean, the calm waters provide an ideal habitat for seabirds, whales, and seals. In the spring when warmer water moves into the area, tuna, mackerel, tropical flying-fish, and sea turtles thrive in the bays.

Beyond Boutiliers Point, following the shore road for 15 km, you pass the warm sand and cool water beaches at **Black Point**, **Queensland**, and **Hubbards**. A km past Hubbards Beach Campground is **Highway 329**. Turn **left** onto the Aspotogan Peninsula. If you need supplies, before you make the turn onto 329 you can find a supermarket 400 meters farther on Highway 3.

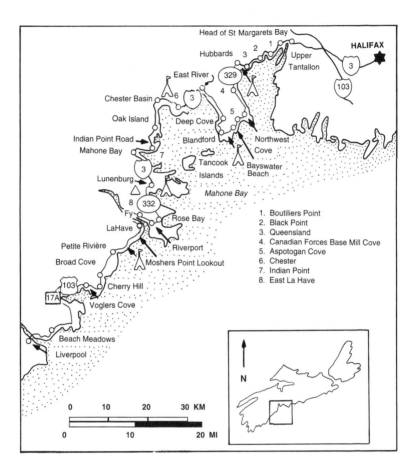

The Aspotogan Peninsula, originally named by the Micmacs for "where they block the passageway for seals," is one of this tour's highlights. The road, almost deserted, dips in and climbs out of small coves. Fishermen still ply these waters, mostly for tuna and mackerel, but not long ago the area supported a thriving whaling industry. Today, the peninsula is within commuting distance to Halifax, allowing city workers to live in and enjoy the area.

About 1 km after the junction with Highway 3, turn **left** toward **Mill Cove**. During another 5 km of quiet, seaside riding, you pass **Canadian Forces Base Mill Cove**, and after another 8 km you pass the idyllic fishing village of **Northwest Cove**. In this small cove look for the large, round tubes used for dying nets. Beyond Northwest Cove the road veers inland over crests that offer views of small lakes. After 4 more km, you pass the photogenic village of **Aspotogan Cove**, a hamlet of less than ten houses, snuggled in the sheltered harbor. Past the village 4 km, you reach windswept **Bayswater Beach and Picnic Area**. After 5 km, you cross over a headland and come to a junction to New Harbour. Continue on **329 right**, and, after 2 km, you reach **Blandford**. This village, originally settled by the Irish in 1750, was the center of the area's whaling industry. Blandford is now a tourist haunt. As you follow this shore road you enjoy extensive views of Mahone Bay and the Tancook Islands. The road creeps inland for 4 km to circle the long arm of **Deep Cove**. Beyond Deep Cove the road follows the coast, but you have fewer seascapes to enjoy. Instead, for 10 km you pass pastureland and farms until you rejoin **Highway 3** at **East River**. The large factory to your right refinishes timber and specializes in making wood siding. Turn **left**. If you chose to forego the peninsula and stay on Highway 3, there are 9 km between Hubbards and East River.

Another 6 km past East River takes you to the junction **left to Graves Island Provincial Park**. This park, situated on an eroded drumlin, is one of the most beautiful in the province. From Highway 3 it's just 1 short km over a causeway to the shaded campsites overlooking Mahone Bay.

Graves Island Provincial Park to Lunenburg: 47.1 kilometers

From **Highway 3** continue **left** for 3 km to **Chester**. The highway bypasses town, but if you want to explore it, you'll find Cape Cod architecture and a quiet atmosphere. New Englanders, up to 1750, sailed from Massachusetts harbors on their way to the fishing banks. Ten years later, New England Planters settled in the area. Now Chester is a summer resort, connected to the Tancook Islands by a ferry.

As you leave Chester, stay on **Highway 3**. Expect heavy traffic for 3 km until you reach the junction for Highway 14. Stay on 3. The road through this area crosses over a few hills, but the grades are comfortable and the traffic is light to moderate. After 5 km, you pass through **Chester Basin** and the intersection to Highway 12, the 25-km road to Ross Farm. Beyond the intersection, expect flat terrain as you ride beside island-sprinkled Mahone Bay. After 6 km, you come to an indistinct intersection leading to mysterious **Oak Island**.

The first record of the findings at Oak Island dates back to 1795 when a hunter noticed a saucer-shaped depression in the ground. Starting to dig, he exposed a layer of logs, but fearing what lay underneath, he abandoned it. In the early 1800s professional miners began systematically exploring the pit. They discovered layers of logs buried at regular intervals. At a level of about 10 meters they struck a large stone slab with a mysterious code deciphered to read "40 feet below two million pounds are buried." When the excited group removed the platform under the rock, water rushed into the pit, killing the miners. The rock barrier had controlled a system of hydraulic seals within an intricate flooding system. Since then, no one has been able to shut off the water. So, what lies buried under Oak Island? Some say the treasure of the Incas, others say pirates used this ideal hiding spot, shielded by the Tancook Islands, to bury their gold. The current theory asserts a group of Royal engineers used Oak Island to cache the funds used to buy supplies and pay troops during the American Revolution. Still, no one has discovered a treasure, but you can visit the island and the visitor center and view an audio-video presentation.

From Oak Island the road bends inland for 5 km to **Indian Point Road**. Turn **left**. For 3 km you follow a wooded section of road with views into Narrows Basin until you reach another junction. To the left is the small village of **Indian Point** with its old houses and panorama of islands. Continue **right** for another 6 km, following the shore of Mahone Harbour. As you near Mahone Bay you'll see one of the most famous scenes of Nova Scotia: three exalted church spires that bless everyone entering town. Once you reach **Highway 3**, turn **left**, and after a short km, you reach **Mahone Bay Tourist Office**. After another 1.5 km, you reach an intersection. Turn **left** continuing on **Highway 3**.

Mahone's name refers to *mahonnes*, a type of low-built pirate ship that once zigzagged through the bay to dodge the British Navy. Today, the town is a cozy little place filled with antique shops, restaurants, and Victorian-era homes. Its one main attraction, the Settlers Museum and Cultural Centre, exhibits ceramics, household goods, and furniture dated between 1790 and 1840.

Follow narrow **Highway 3**, out of town along the shore. After 3 km, leave the harbor and cross over a few small hills. After another 7 km, turn **left** at the junction with **Highway 323** and after another 200 meters turn **right** on **3**, also known as **Maple Street**, which veers **left** and becomes **Dufferin Street**; after another 400 meters, it becomes **Lincoln Street**. Stay **left** and be careful of the STOP sign at the bottom of the hill. Passing through downtown another km, turn **left** at **Blockhouse Hill**. Voilà, you have reached the **Lunenburg Board of Trade Campground**.

Lunenburg to Liverpool: 73 kilometers

Lunenburg enchants visitors with its historic, scenic, and cultural beauty. Initially, the Micmacs used the site as a summer encampment. Later, it was a French fishing harbor, but it wasn't until 1751 that French, German, and Swiss immigrants cleared the area for farmland and founded the city of Lunenburg. The best way to become familiar with the history and architecture is to join one of the guided tours that the Historical Society of Lunenburg offers during the summer. As you wander through town, delight in the flashy reds, subdued blues, and blazing yellows of the painted homes and buildings. Notice the different architectural styles: overhanging windows, elaborate towers, cornices, pilaster capitals, and intricate filigree work. Fishing crews, headed toward the Grand Banks, wiled away their boredom by carving the rich woodwork now adorning the homes.

Housed in the red warehouses downtown, the Fisheries Museum of the Atlantic offers an overview of the North Atlantic fishing industry.

A small dory sits on the inky waters of Lunenburg harbor.

Upon entering, you find aquariums holding native fish: Atlantic cod, known as the "King of the Sea," and electric eels clumped and slithering together like Medusa's hair. Beyond the aquariums, the museum displays fishing techniques, dory building, and the history of rum running and documents the current problems of the Grand Banks Fishery. You can also climb aboard two ships, *Teresa E. Connor*, a schooner outfitted as a working ship (notice the chalkboard listing the sailors' meals), and *Cape Sable*, a steel-hulled trawler that once harvested cod. Visiting the Fisheries Museum is an informative way to spend part of a day, especially if fog has blanketed the town.

The origin of the term *Bluenose* is contentious. One theory states the term refers to the Loyalists who arrived from the American Revolution and whose loyalty was "true blue." Another theory states the name derives from a species of potato with bluish eyes that locals ate with salted herring. Yet another theory states that fishermen in the area, bound for the offshore banks, painted the bows of their dories a bright blue.

Leaving the campground at Lunenburg, cycle straight down **Cumberland Street** toward downtown. After 500 meters turn **left** on **King Street**, 100 meters farther turn **right** on **Pelham Street**, and 100 meters farther still, merge with **Lincoln Street**. Follow Lincoln for 500 meters, then turn **left** on **Falkland Street**. After another 200 meters turn **right** on **Victoria Street**. Finally, leaving Lunenburg after 2.2 km, take **Highway 332 West** to **Rose Bay**. If it's foggy, listen for the foghorn moaning like a heartbroken mother who has lost her children at sea. After 12 km, you come to the junction for the Ovens, 3.5 km down the side road. The Ovens are sea caves carved by the tides. Micmac lore tells that it was possible to paddle a canoe into one of the openings and come out on the Fundy coast on the other side of Nova Scotia.

Beyond this junction 2 km, you pass **Riverport**. Beyond town 1 km, turn **right** over the bridge, following **Highway 332**. After the bridge, veer **left**, from where you will see the small town of LaHave across the LaHave River. After about 3 km, you ride along the coast past pine forest, and then you arrive at the **East LaHave Ferry**. The ferry operates from 6:00 A.M. to midnight, leaving East LaHave every hour on the half hour and returning from LaHave on the hour. The trip is free for bikes and walk-on passengers. After crossing on the ferry, turn **left** on **37W**. You are now at **LaHave**, a still town with deep history.

The French explorer, de Monts, arrived in LaHave in 1604, and named the site Cap de la Havre, meaning "The Harbor." But it wasn't until 1632 that the French established a settlement and named it Fort Marie de Grâce after the patron saint of their arrival date. Today, the intimate atmosphere and romantic coastal scenery attract artists and craftspeople. You can also visit the Fort Point Museum, the former lighthouse keeper's home; it commemorates the first landing of the Acadians in 1632.

Past LaHave 3 km, continuing on **Highway 332**, you come upon **Moshers Point Lookout** where small wharves slip out from shore and moored trawlers gaze onto the open sea. This road offers some of the most beautiful oceanfront riding on the South Shore. On the right, farmers try growing root crops, and, to supplement their income, they also fish for lobster and carve wood. Lobster pots sit stacked on the roadside, and a carved model boat may be sitting in a garage waiting to be finished.

After 8 km, the oceanfront riding ends and you reach **Rissers Provincial Park**, offering camping, the best stretch of sand beach in Nova Scotia, and a walkway over a salt marsh. **Petite Rivière** appears after another 2 km. The French named the spot "Little River" to distinguish it from the larger LaHave River. Another 0.5 km farther leads to a steep uphill through heavy forest. Extensive views overlook the pine-covered hills of the Atlantic Uplands. The next 7 km feel like the tour's most isolated section. You won't find any farms or cottages until you reach **Broad Cove**. Beyond this village you follow an open sea of drumming waves and tiny fishing outposts hugging the shore until you come to **Cherry Hill**, 4 km farther. You arrive at **Voglers Cove** after 6.5 km. After another 16 km through dense forest, you reach **Highway 103**. Bear **left** on this main highway. If you want to avoid this short stretch of highway, continue straight and circle back onto Medway Road. Follow 103 for 2 km and exit carefully **left** on **Exit 17A**. You pass more dense forest and marshes along this slightly hilly route. For the next 16 km you pass the junction to Port Medway and to East Berlin Road. Keep **right**. When you reach **Beach Meadows**, turn **left** along **Brooklyn Shore Road**. You will find a slight urban buildup as you ride along this area, and after another 6 km you rejoin **Highway 3**. Turn **left** over the bridge. After another 3 km of urban riding, you reach the junction with **Highway 8**, and the continuation of Tour No. 3. A km more takes you into downtown Liverpool.

TOUR NO. 3

RAPPIE, KEDJIE, AND DORIES

Start / Finish: Yarmouth/Yarmouth
Distance: 615.5 kilometers (383 miles)
Estimated time: 7 days
Terrain: Flat to rolling
Map: Nova Scotia—The Doer's and
Dreamer's Complete Map
Connecting tours: Tour Nos. 2 and 5
Connections: Ferries from Bar Harbor, Maine, and
Portland, Maine, connect to Yarmouth;
also from St. John, New Brunswick, to
Digby; also Highways 101 and 103 and
Yarmouth International Airport

The historical French Shore, birdwatching, and the Atlantic's only inland national park fill Nova Scotia's longest tour. The route begins at historical Yarmouth and then passes a crucial center of Acadian culture. Clare County, Kejimkujik National Park, Western Head, and Cape Sable Island offer the patient bicycle tourist outstanding scenery, wildlife, and the Acadian and Loyalist traditions of Nova Scotia. Plan to spend time in unique Kejimkujik National Park (Kedjie) and bustling Cape Sable Island. Relax and enjoy the tour; the history and scenery are worth savoring.

Most of the tour follows secondary roads, although there are parts where you have to ride on the main highway. Not to worry though, as these sections are well paved and have shoulders. If you want to shorten parts of the tour, skip any of the headlands by detouring onto the main highways. Food is generally easy to find except for isolated stretches on Route 8 and on the coastal headlands. You can find bike shops at Yarmouth, Digby, Shelburne, and Barrington Passage.

The French Shore Road (Highway 1), paralleling the unprotected coast, can be very windy due to the funneling of air currents between the mainland and Digby neck. Periodically, the south shore can be foggy. The interior of Nova Scotia maintains a distinct climate compared to the rest of Nova Scotia. Lower rainfall and higher summer temperatures offer a unique environment for plants and animals found nowhere else north of the southern United States.

Yarmouth to Church Point: 71 kilometers

Yarmouth, sitting at Nova Scotia's southwestern edge, maintains a strong seafaring tradition. The first Europeans to arrive in the area

A statue of Jesus stands beside St. Mary's Church at Church Point.

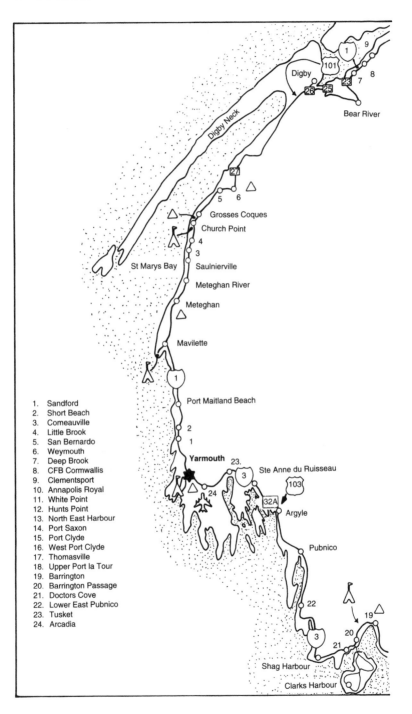

1. Sandford
2. Short Beach
3. Comeauville
4. Little Brook
5. San Bernardo
6. Weymouth
7. Deep Brook
8. CFB Cormwallis
9. Clementsport
10. Annapolis Royal
11. White Point
12. Hunts Point
13. North East Harbour
14. Port Saxon
15. Port Clyde
16. West Port Clyde
17. Thomasville
18. Upper Port la Tour
19. Barrington
20. Barrington Passage
21. Doctors Cove
22. Lower East Pubnico
23. Tusket
24. Arcadia

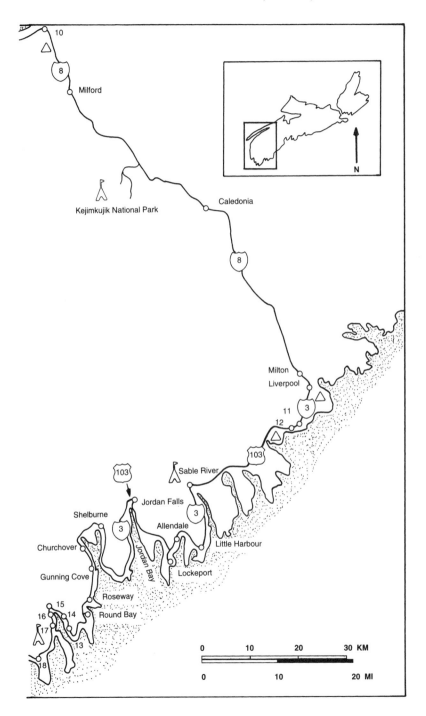

were sixteenth-century fishermen who used the sheltered site to wait out the Atlantic Ocean's ferocious storms. Samuel de Champlain, in 1604, was the first European to describe the area and only twenty-three years later the French were using Yarmouth's natural harbor as a fur-trading post. Yet it was not until the New England "planters" set out to "plant" a New England after the Acadian expulsion that Yarmouth became a settlement. In 1870, the city reached its zenith as a Maritimes shipbuilding center. Legends and tales recount the city's days of glory and its subsequent decline at the advent of the steamship. Because of Yarmouth's convenient location as a stopover between Boston and Europe, the town did maintain its status as a maritime center. Today, the ferries, now larger than anyone could have imagined then, shuttle between Maine and Yarmouth.

You begin the tour in downtown **Yarmouth** at the corner of **Main** and **Forest streets**. From this intersection, the tourist office and the ferry terminal are directly in front of you. Cycling to your right about 1 km through moderate city traffic (passing the Firefighter's Museum), turn **left** onto **304 South (Vancouver Street)**. You'll recognize the turn by the small bronze horse to the left. After another km of some short hills, you come to a Y intersection. To the left is Highway 304 South, to the right, **Sandford Road**.

If you continued south on 304 you would pass salt marshes and scrub land and Cape Forchu Wharf with its large breakwater and walls of lobster pots, and after 6 km, you would arrive at the rock perch of the Cape Forchu Light Station.

Stay on Sandford Road and cross open farmland until you reach the village of **Sandford** about 7 km farther. Look for North America's smallest operating drawbridge, built during the First World War. As you leave the town, notice the views of High Head's gray cliffs rising out of the Atlantic's inky blue waters. After another 5 km, you pass the settlement of **Short Beach** and small Allen's Lake and reach the junction to **Highway 1** posted as the **Evangeline Trail**. Turn **left** in the direction of Halifax. Following the shores of **Lake Darling**, the route begins to roll and the road becomes a little steeper. About 3 km farther, you reach **Port Maitland Beach**. Another 13 km of continuous rolling hills with some short, steep sections take you to **Mavilette**. A half km to the left is **Mavilette Beach Provincial Park**.

After Mavilette, you enter Clare County, known locally as the French Shore. Passing through the county, you experience extensive views over the Atlantic, more beaches, and small fishing villages hunkering on the small headlands.

The history of the Acadians during the seventeenth century accounts for the proud culture that exists today on the French Shore. First the successful settlers were expulsed in 1755, and the British forced the unfortunate exiles to relocate throughout eastern North America, some as far as Louisiana, where they became known as "Cajuns," and back to France, where they were foreigners. Several years later, as political tensions between France and England eased, some of the Acadians returned but found the rich farmlands that they had wrestled from the sea occupied by New Englanders. Some of the wandering Acadians finally resettled on the French Shore.

Today, in Clare County, the Acadian influence remains distinct and intense. Most of the population is bilingual, the tri-colored red, white, and blue flags emblazoned with a gold star on its corner still fly from many homes, and *pâté a la rapure*, "rappie pie," a traditional meal of fried, glazed, and baked potato and chicken, is served as the region's culinary specialty.

A string of twelve communities, the French Shore stretches for 40 km along the coast. The road begins rolling through sections of forest and then levels out to gentle farmland. After 11 km you reach **Smugglers Cove Provincial Park**—a great rest spot. Providing a tourist office, picnic tables, and an outhouse, the site overlooks the cove's dramatic cliffs.

Down the road 1 km is **Meteghan**. This small village is home to *La Vieille Maison*, a typical museum/house depicting the lifestyle of the nineteenth-century Acadians. During the summer, guides dressed in traditional costume display the house and gardens.

Through the towns of the French Shore the road widens to include a full, paved shoulder. Watch out for "Digby rubbernecking"; it happens when you gaze around at the seascapes and towns until—wham!—you get jolted by a sewer grate embedded in the road's shoulder. Traffic intensifies, but drivers are courteous and they will usually slow down rather than trying to squeeze past you.

After **Meteghan River** (another 6 km), you pass through the towns of **Saulnierville**, **Comeauville**, and **Little Brook**. Along the route you'll see St. Mary's Church perched on **Church Point**. After 14 km you reach the town, known in the area as **Pointe de l'Eglise.**

After 14 km, you arrive at St. Mary's Church, which has been beckoning you from its perch on the landscape. The church was constructed between 1903 and 1905 and holds the title of being North America's largest wooden church. The seemingly fantasy-inspired tower rises 56 meters, and because of the strong winds coming off the bay 36 tons of rock were placed in the spire to act as ballast.

Church Point has full provisions, including a supermarket, a bed and breakfast, and a campground.

Church Point to Annapolis Royal: 94 kilometers

The road flattens out after Church Point and traffic decreases to make the ride feel more relaxing. About 5 km along is **Grosses Coques** (Large Clams), a small town of 357. The original Acadians named this small settlement after they survived their first winter by eating the area's scallops. Just past the **Grosses Coques River Bridge** is an optional left junction to Major Point Bridge, which leads to the site of the first Acadian cemetery. A cairn and small chapel mark the site.

After 13 km you arrive in **San Bernardo** (St. Bernard), where you can see the Gothic church of St. Anne. The locals took thirty-two years to complete this huge, granite structure, finally laying the last stone in

A trawler gets refitted at the dry docks of Little Brook.

1942. Just 2 km beyond this village you pass **under Highway 101**; staying on **Route 1**, you reach **Weymouth**.

The United Empire Loyalists settled in Weymouth in 1783. This disenfranchised group of New Englanders remained loyal to the British Crown during the American Revolution. In the colonies a Loyalist was "a thing whose head is in England and whose body is in America and whose neck ought to be stretched."

The Weymouth Historical Society houses a museum in St. Thomas Anglican Church.

Continue through Weymouth, **straight up** the hill along **Highway 1**. After about 3 km, you reach **Exit 27** on **Highway 101 East**. Continue on the **right** along **101** to Digby. Highway 101 is decent but banal. This two-lane highway, gliding up and down through some long hills, does boast a 1-meter paved shoulder. Notice Digby Neck with its red cliffs and whitewashed towns across the bay. Be careful of the bridge joints at the bottoms of hills and the gravel spilling over from driveways along the highway. Past the exit 7 km, you reach **Savary Picnic Park**, overlooking Digby Neck's cliffs. Another 15 km and you come to **Exit 26** to **Digby**. At the bottom of the exit, turn **left** following **303 South**. If you want to avoid visiting Digby, continue straight on 101. This road to Digby has a shoulder, but be careful of the nasty drops into the sewer grates. After 3 km you come to a junction for the ferry to St. John, New Brunswick. Continue **straight** to downtown **Digby**. After about 1 km you reach a steep downhill. After 1 more short km you arrive in downtown Digby.

Admiral Digby captained the first flotilla of 1,500 Loyalist refugees who began settling in the area. If you want to delve further into the town's history, you can visit the Admiral Digby Museum, which contains photographs and a map room. Alternatively, if you want to drag for scallops, fish for tuna, and learn about the fishing industry first-hand, a tour operator offers half-day excursions.

Digby remains headquarters of the Digby Scallop Fleet, and although the stocks have been depleted in recent years, the dragging crews still harvest some of the world's best scallops. Interestingly, the Prohibition rum runners of the 1920s found the area's finest scallop bays. Forced to seek harbor from bad weather or to hide from the American Coast Guard, the smugglers used their idle time to—what else?—drag for scallops.

Returning to **Exit 26**, continue for about 3 km along **101 East** to **Exit 25**. At the turnoff for **Joggin Bridge** turn **left** on **Landsdowne Road** to **Bear River**. After 7 km on this road you come to Bear River Hill, a steep 1.5-km drop with two tight curves. You could easily exceed the posted 50-kph speed limit. At the bottom of the hill you arrive in **Bear River**.

Hills surround this small settlement that Nova Scotians loosely refer to as "Little Switzerland." Pretty it is—but Switzerland? Anyway, the location of the village has attracted a small arts community specializing in some unique crafts.

Continuing the tour, before you head into town and cross the bridge turn **left** along **Old River Road**. This rolling road follows the small escarpment along Bear River and offers glimpses of the waterway and surrounding hills. After 7 km take the on-ramp for **101 East**. After another 500 meters you reach **Smith Cove Lookout**. You should walk the short trail to the lookout to admire the surrounding views.

Return to **101 East** and continue **right**. Take a quick downhill over Bear River Bridge and climb for another kilometer, passing views over the Digby Basin and a lighthouse, to **Exit 23**. Take the exit **right** to **Cornwallis**; you are now on **Highway 1 East**.

This highway rolls through **Deep Brook**, **Canadian Forces Base Cornwallis**, and **Clementsport**. Traffic through this section is moderate, but it could be busy on weekends when people drive out to the amusement park. From Exit 23 it is 23 km **to Upper Clements Wildlife Park**. The park contains two walking trails and displays animals indigenous to Nova Scotia.

Past the park 6 km, the Victorian town of **Annapolis Royal** provides bed and breakfasts, a campground, supermarkets, and a number of attractions. (See Tour No. 4 for details on Annapolis Royal.)

Annapolis Royal to Kejimkujik National Park: 63 kilometers

At the town's entrance is the junction for **Highway 8 South**. Turning **right**, facing the direction you arrived in Annapolis Royal, follow the "paddler" symbol. Highway 8 offers a gently rolling, forested landscape dotted with lakes and streams. At 3 km past the junction, you reach the turn to **Lequille Power Plant and Historic Site**. The attraction is a power station disguised as a seventeenth-century grist mill.

From the power plant cycle another 44 km to the entrance **of Kejimkujik National Park**. Plan to spend the rest of the day exploring the park's walking and cycling trails. If you stop at the **Interpretive Centre**, just 1 km into the park, the staff will give you a map outlining the available cycling trails. The day's tour ends 16 km into the park at the full-service **campground**. You won't find any food except at the campground's canteen, so pick up supplies at Maitland Bridge before entering the park. If you don't want to or can't camp, Milford, 23 km back north, and Caledonia, 16 km farther south, offer formal lodging.

Kejimkujik National Park to Liverpool: 71.3 kilometers

From the campground at Kejimkujik, return to the park entrance and turn **right** on **Highway 8**. The road south to Liverpool rolls and winds between the forests, lakes, and hills. Geologists call the area's hills drumlins. Formed during the last ice age, the tear-shaped hills are composed of the clay and rock material deposited by receding glaciers. Down the road 16 km you come to a Y intersection at **Caledonia**. Keep **left** following the "paddler" of **Highway 8 South**. The isolated, scenic road levels out as you pass by lakes, bogs, and picnic areas. After 44 km you pass through the town of **Milton**. Beyond Milton 3 km you reach the city of **Liverpool**, which offers accommodations and supermarkets.

At Liverpool you can pick up a self-guided walking tour booklet at the town's tourist office. The tour boasts the Victorian homes commissioned by the area's long-dead sea captains, shipbuilders, and lumber merchants.

During the nineteenth century, Liverpool took advantage of its easy access, by way of the Mersey River, to thousands of acres of forest. The city became a major shipbuilding center, but as the settlers depleted the forests and the wooden ship era ended, the town declined. In the 1920s pulp and paper became the town's main industry, and the Bowater-Mersey pulp and paper mill, unsightly as it may be, is still the town's biggest employer.

Liverpool to Shelburne: 129 kilometers

If you find this day's ride too long or portions too taxing, you can skip any of the headlands and stay on shorter, more direct, but less scenic Highway 101. This ride follows some of the most isolated headlands of the South Shore. Before you enter these capes, stock up on food, as you will find only a couple of convenience stores.

Leaving Liverpool is tricky, but by following the signs for **Highway 3 South**, navigating is easy. At the junction to **Highway 3 South**, ride 1 km to reach **Main Street**. Liverpool's two museums are toward the left, but turn **right** on Main. After another 0.5 km turn **left** on **Panzant Road**. Up the road 400 meters **at White Point Road (Highway 3)** turn **right**, leaving Liverpool.

The terrain beyond town is level and traffic is light except for the weekends when the sun-loving Nova Scotians trek to the area's beaches and resorts. Stay on **Highway 3** for the next 11 km, passing **White Point** and **Hunts Point**. Along this route, cottages pepper the roadside and you can enjoy the views of the sea and boulders. After another 4 km, you reach **Summerville Beach Park**, a long, beckoning sandy beach that unfortunately offers only frigid dips into the ocean. About 1.5 km past the park you reach the junction to **Highway 103**. Turn **left** onto **103 West** toward Shelburne. Highway 103, although hilly, has a good shoulder and moderate traffic. No alternate roads parallel the highway, so you must cycle this short section. After 3.5 km, you reach the junction to **Port Mouton**, named by the explorer de Monts when a sheep jumped overboard from his ship.

Another 9 km down Highway 103 is the junction to **Port Joli**.

Back on Highway 103, the road rises and drops between ridges. If you thought Nova Scotia was a flat land of rocks, climbing these pine-covered hills will dispel that myth. After 15 km you enter the district of **Sable River** and pass a derelict grist mill, then 0.5 km past a campground you turn left at the junction for **Highway 3**. The road now follows the shore of the Sable River estuary. This level and quiet road becomes even more quiet after 4 km when you turn **left** on **Coves Head Road**. You pass the settlement of **Little Harbour**. Riding past the spruce and fir forest, punctuated by farmhouses and cottages, you catch occasional glimpses of the Atlantic Ocean. After 19 km, you reach the junction to **Highway 3 West**. Turn left, rejoining the trunk road. The route becomes more hilly, passing the village of **Allendale**. After 6 km, you arrive at the junction for **Lockeport**. **Highway 3** continues **right**.

To the left 4 km, along Lockeport Road, lies the town of Lockeport, a scenic town built on an island and connected to the mainland by a sand causeway. Lockeport is an interesting town and, like many of the towns of the South Shore, was settled by the New England migrations of 1750. During the American Revolution, privateers habitually raided the seaside towns. In one incident, the women of the town spotted an American privateer closing in on the village. Most of the town's males were out at the fishing grounds. So, the town's women were left to defend the settlement. Arming themselves with muskets and draping their shoulders in bright red shawls, they fooled the privateers into thinking British soldiers were guarding the town. The privateers quickly sailed away, sparing the town. Today, you can visit the Little School Museum, Lockeport's first schoolhouse, which the residents built in 1845. The small house holds artifacts and a replica of an early schoolroom.

Continuing back on Highway 3 West, you roll through a wooded, isolated area with views of **Jordan Bay**. After about 17 km, you reach the junction of **Highway 103**. Turn **left**, crossing the bridge to **Jordan Falls**. Be careful crossing the main highway. After less than 1 km, turn **left** on **Jordan Bay Road**. Jordan Falls has a grocery store and restaurant, so stock up, as the next headland, **Western Head**, offers no provisions. If you want to avoid the noisy traffic of the main highway, 5 km along Jordan Bay Road is an intersection that in 6 km will reach Shelburne. Also, if due to fatigue or time you choose to cycle over only one headland, choose Western Head. The route opens to gorgeous views over forested ridges, and as you reach the headland's end, you can view the Atlantic Ocean and McNutt Island. The road, lonely and windswept, has only a few cottages and farmhouses set back in the woods. On the western side of the head the road levels out and hugs Shelburne Harbour. **Shelburne** slides into view as you pass along the rocky shore peppered with fish stores, small docks, and a lighthouse. From Jordan Falls the Western Head route continues for 31 km until you arrive in **Shelburne**. Turn **left** on **George Street**, and after 300 meters, turn **right** on **Water Street**, passing Courtney House (1784) on the right corner. In 600 meters you arrive at the junction to **103**. The tourist office and historic district are 100 meters to your left. Shelburne offers full provisions, including a provincial park and campground.

Shelburne to Barrington Passage: 91 kilometers

Loyalist founders settled Shelburne in 1783. Because the British encouraged settlers to migrate to the area, Shelburne's population escalated to 10,000, becoming the largest town in the British North American colonies. Although Shelburne's harbor was excellent, farmers found it impossible to cultivate the rocky, infertile soil. Since food was difficult to grow, most of the population eventually moved to other Loyalist settlements.

Dock Street, on Shelburne's waterfront, houses a museum complex, including the Dory Shop, where dory builders demonstrate how they make these inshore fishing boats. Ross Thompson House, built in 1784, is a re-creation of a Loyalist store and home. Filled with fragrances of rope, molasses, and spices, it's worth a visit. Finally, the Shelburne County Museum documents and exhibits Shelburne County's history.

From the junction at Highway 103 in downtown Shelburne at the corners of **King Street** and **Water Street**, continue **north** for 1.2 km and veer **left** on **Falls Lane**. After another 500 meters, turn **left** on

McGills Point Road (Highway 3 West). Pass the junction for Island Park Picnic and Campground. Continuing straight, cross a long hill out of Shelburne. Since Highway 3 parallels 103, traffic is light. Follow a quiet, wooded road, and after about 5.5 km, turn **left** on **Gunning Cove Road**. If you were to continue straight, you would end up at 103 West.

The road begins to roll. After about 3 km, you arrive at **Churchover** (no provisions). You can spot Shelburne Bay, and if you look back you see Shelburne across the shore. This is the tour's most isolated section. The road continues to undulate between tidal marshes and 200-meter-long climbs. Over the next section you pass the village districts of **Gunning Cove**, **Roseway**, **Round Bay**, **North East Harbour**, **Port Saxon**, and **Port Clyde**. None of these districts offers provisions. Watch for the views of open sea, tidal marshes, and Ingomar across North East Harbour Bay. After 35 kilometers, you reach the junction to the collector road for 103. Turn **left**, in the opposite direction, over the bridge, following Highway 3 to **Port la Tour**. Beyond the bridge 0.5 km you come to **West Port Clyde**, the first general store for 35 km. Beyond Clyde River you travel 5 km, over mostly rocky marsh, to reach the tree-lined streets and whitewashed houses of **Thomasville**. Beyond this little village 8 km, you reach **Upper Port la Tour**, and 3 km farther you arrive at the junction to **Baccaro**.

At the intersection turn **right**, crossing some desolate scrub land. After 7 km you reach **Sandhill Beach Provincial Park**. This extensive park contains various ecological systems, including salt marsh, tidal estuary, sand pit, barrier beach, cranberry marsh, and large sand dune. You might be able to swim at the beach when the incoming tide flows across the warmed sands; otherwise the water is freezing. If you explore the trails, don't walk off them as you may destabilize the dunes and vegetation. After 4.5 km, you come to the junction with 3 West. Veer **left** to **Barrington** (campground). Traffic volume increases and the shoulder is unpaved, so take extra care. After 1.5 km, you arrive on the edge of town at the Old Woolen Mill Museum.

Just over the bridge is the tourist office, and after another 1.5 km you reach the short road to Seal Island Lighthouse Museum. Although the lighthouse is a replica from Seal Island, 80 km offshore from Shag Harbour, you can visit the lighthouse, browse though its artifacts, and climb five stories to view the surrounding area. If you are lucky, you might meet Walter Hichens, a volunteer guide whose great-great-grandparents founded and lived at the original lighthouse at Seal Island.

Past the lighthouse 1 km is a junction for 103 West, but you continue **straight** on **Highway 3**. Another 5 km past the junction you reach **Barrington Passage**, which has full provisions.

Barrington Passage to Yarmouth: 86.5 kilometers

From the edge of Barrington Passage you arrive at the junction to **Highway 330 South**.

To follow this 40-km journey that encircles Cape Sable Island, follow

303 South and cross the causeway. Fishing villages, sand beaches, fish plants, sea scenery, and a boatbuilding industry ring the island. The circumnavigation route is mostly level, easy cycling. Since most cyclists like milestones, make note that Hawk Point is the most southerly point in Nova Scotia. Strong winds sometimes blow across the causeway, so be careful.

After about 1.2 km past the museum, you reach the junction to Stoney Point. Continue on 303. After 6.5 km, you reach **Clarks Harbour**. Out to the right you'll see the lighthouse at Hawk Point. The southern portion of the island is a windswept place providing an austere environment for boat builders.

Past Clarks Harbour 4.5 km you come to Hawk Road, which leads, naturally, to Hawk Point. This short, 2.5-km one-way road to the right crosses tidal marshes and a lonely settlement. Following **303 North** on the eastern side of the island you cross more forest as the road turns inland. Through some sections you can see Baccaro Point and radar station. After 6 km, you arrive back at the junction, follow it **right** for 200 meters, and turn right again on Stoney Island Road. The eastern section of the island is less developed due to its distance from the sea. After 4 km, you reach Stoney Island, and after another 7 km, the road ends. Continue **right** on 303 North back over the causeway.

Continuing straight on **3 West** through the small village of **Doctors Cove**, after 9.5 km, you arrive at **Chapel Hill Museum and Observation Tower** at **Shag Harbour**. From the hill in town on a clear night you can spot five light stations, evidence of the coast's dangerous fogs, low-lying islands, reefs, and ledges. The road however, is slightly rolling, passing by lighthouses and lobster-processing plants. After 13 km, you come to the junction of **Forbes Point**, climb over a rise out of Woods Harbour District, and arrive in the Pubnico District. After 2 km, you pass a sea-plant cultivation area where they grow Irish moss, which is used as a natural coagulator in gelatin. After another 4 km, you arrive at **Lower East Pubnico**. In this area a mere seven villages share the name Pubnico.

While you cycle through the area, keep a lookout for Irish moss being spread out to dry. The road rolls through the **Eastern Pubnico District** for 15.5 km, leading to an intersection that accesses Highway 103. Turn **left** following **Highway 3**. **Pubnico** quickly follows in 800 meters. At this point you reach the junction to 355 that follows the West Pubnico District. Turn **right** on **3 West** to **Argyle**. For 14 km, following a small ridge over farmlands and woods, you may enjoy the views over Old Point Channel and Argyle River. At the next junction keep **left** toward 103. After another 400 meters you reach **103**. Turn **right** on the two-lane divided highway with a paved shoulder. Be careful crossing the bridges as the shoulder virtually disappears. After 1.2 km exit on **32A** back onto **Highway 3 West** to Greenwood. Follow **Bayside Road** through flat, forested countryside for 8 km to **Ste. Anne du Ruisseau**.

Notice the heavy French influence in the area in the predominantly

French names and Acadian flags. In another 4 km, you reach the junction for Amiraut's Hill and Morris Island.

At this junction is the **Hanging Oak Antique and Craft Shop**. Once an old country store, it has remained in the same family for generations. Locals, circumventing the nearby courthouse, once used the hanging oak as a crude gallows. Past this junction 400 meters is **Tusket**, and facing the road is Canada's oldest courthouse. Built in 1805, locals continued to use it until 1976. Today you can visit the courtroom, judges' chambers, and jail cells. After you cycle past Tusket, keep **left** to see cattle, apple trees, and roadside stands selling smoked kippers and herring. The pleasant farm scenery is complemented by little traffic and flat to gently rolling terrain. Past Tusket 9 km is Yarmouth's campground and another 2 km down the road is **Arcadia**. Beyond Arcadia 2 km, on **3 West**, traffic picks up as you pass **Yarmouth Airport**. At the first set of lights on **Hardscratch Road**, turn **left**. Another km farther, turn **right** on **Forest Road**, and after 2 km, you are at the corner of **Main** and **Forest streets**, the tourist office, and the ferry terminal.

TOUR NO. 4

ANNAPOLIS VALLEY

Start / Finish: Annapolis Royal/Windsor
Distance: 187 kilometers (114 miles)
Estimated time: 3 days
Terrain: Flat to rolling with a few severe hills
Map: Nova Scotia—The Doer's and
Dreamer's Complete Map
Connecting tours: Tour No. 3
Connections: Digby Ferry to St. John, New
Brunswick; Highway 101

The Annapolis Valley was once the most fought-over piece of territory in North America. Set between the North Mountains and the South Hills, it served as the backdrop for the French-Anglo struggle for North American supremacy. During the long conflict, neither side capitulated. Massacred soldiers, pillaged settlements left in ashes, a town that saw its victor's flag change numerous times, and the heaviest black mark in Canadian history—the Acadian expulsion—were the results of their struggles. Micmac, French, British, Acadian, and New England blood have soaked the valley's soil. Today, as you cycle along the pastoral back roads, the history of bloodletting and violence is almost inconceivable. What were once Micmac settlements are now towns brimming with Victorian homes and art galleries. What was once an Acadian settlement is now a military anti-submarine training base. And what was once the site of the forced exodus of an entire culture is now Nova Scotia's second most visited tourist site. So, here's to the English and the French, the "Redcoats" and the "Cajuns," the Micmacs and the freed slaves. Here's to a past that the fruit trees and pastures have covered but not forgotten.

The Annapolis Valley offers you the best combination of ease and satisfaction. The majority of its route traces the Annapolis and Cornwallis Rivers, passing small farms, orchards, and intimate communities. But before the tour skips lazily past cattle and apple trees, it follows a rigorous route from Annapolis Royal to Port Royal and then over the North Mountain's lip to the Bay of Fundy coast. Then, once you return from the North Mountains and start traveling on the quiet valley roads, you may think you are in bicycle-touring heaven.

Four routes cross the area. The main highway, 101, is convenient, boring, and fast. Don't bother to bicycle on this route. Highway 1, the local crowded highway, cuts through all the major towns. The two minor roads, 202 and 221, offer the best cycling: solitude, rolling terrain, interest, and scenery. Traffic is light, except the stretch between

The Blockhouse, one of Canada's oldest original structures that is still intact, stands outside the city of Windsor.

Wolfville and Kentville, which you can avoid by zigzagging along Highway 341. These minor roads bypass most communities in the valley, so riding to town usually means a 2- to 5-km detour. You can find bike shops at Wolfville and Kingston.

Due to the inversion effect of the flanking mountains, the valley is drier and warmer than on the neighboring coast. Winds generally prevail from the west in the valley and from the southwest on the Fundy shore. The valley averages fifty-five more sunny days per year than the rest of the Maritimes.

Annapolis Royal to Valleyview Provincial Park: 55 kilometers

The tour begins in **Annapolis Royal**, at the corner of **Prince Albert Road** (Highway 1) and **Saint George Street** (Highway 8). The first thing you notice about the town is the expansive Victorian homes festooned with turrets, bay windows, and encircling verandas. If each home could retell its stories, you would hear about a time when the town's docks were chaotic. Apples, lumber, and potatoes were loaded on ships headed to England, Europe, and the United States, while sugar, spices, and rum were unloaded from ships returning from the West Indies. Packet boats, destined for Digby, Saint John, and Boston, stopped to pick up mail transferred by Pony Express. Weary stagecoach drivers hitched their steeds in the stables, and passengers

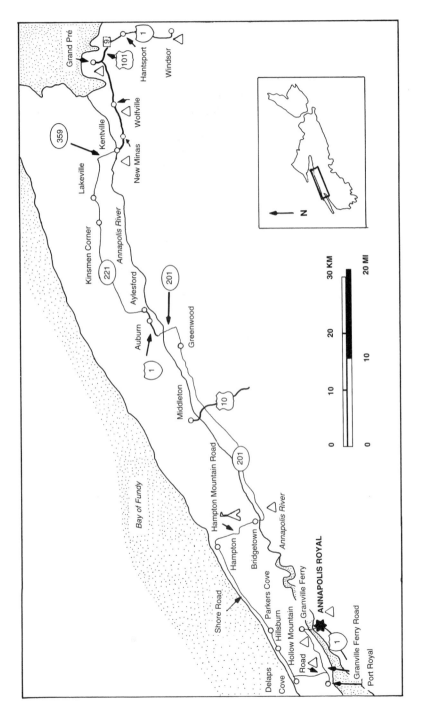

settled down to a warm meal and a cozy bed in the inn to nurse their battered bodies.

Today, as you cycle toward downtown, you pass Canada's oldest historic site, **Fort Anne**. The complex is worth visiting. It consists of earthwork fortifications, the 1708 gunpowder magazine, and the 1797 British field officers' quarters, which now displays the interior woodwork of the original building and documents the Anglo-French struggle.

Saint George Street, originally called Rue Dauphin by the French, passes along the waterfront. In the summer, traffic bustles as you cruise through the tiny downtown business area, containing Odell Tavern (1869), Robertson McNamara House (1785), Adams-Ritchie House (1712), and the oldest wooden house in Canada, de Gannes-Cosby House (1708). All of these buildings are small museums, each of them offering glimpses into the life and times of Annapolis Royal's heyday.

After about 200 meters, you reach the end of St. George Street. Turn **right** onto **Chapel Street**, and then after about another 100 meters, turn **left** onto **Anthony Street**. Before merging onto **Prince Albert Street**, which turns into **Highway 1**, you pass two grocery stores, so stock up here for the day. In another km you cross over the Annapolis River and pass the Tidal Generating Station.

North America's only tidal generating station, producing 20,000 kilowatts of electricity, draws its power from the Fundy tides. At the interpretive center you can see videos, displays, and the station's internal workings. If you have any engineering inclination, the center is worth inspecting.

Another 0.5 km down Highway 1, turn **left** at **Habitation Road**, and after cycling for another km, you pass through the town of **Granville Ferry**. Bringing character to the town, houses date back to 1790. "Entertainment House," a former inn from 1849, was once used by Pony Express riders. When you leave the quiet town the route follows the same path the riders used to carry messages between Victoria Beach and Halifax, where ocean steamers then took the mail onward. Past Granville Ferry 2 km, you pass the **North Hills Museum**, a provincial landmark displaying Georgian furniture, ceramics, glass, and silver. Past the museum you continue along slightly rolling farmland overlooking the Annapolis Basin. After 8 km, you reach **Port Royal National Historic Site**. From the parking lot the fort seems like a gray wall of faded posts, but as you approach the perimeter wall, the steep gabled roofs covered in rough-hewn shingles, tall stone chimneys, studded oak doors, and the palisade armed with its tiny cannons make their presence known. Imagine the bloodshed the walls have seen when fighting was hand to hand and the fear of death gripped each soldier and Micmac warrior. When you enter the fort, a guide, dressed in period costume, introduces himself and recounts the fort's history. Meanwhile, you can admire the buildings facing onto the courtyard, designed similarly to the traders' homeland of Normandy, France.

Returning along **Granville Ferry Road**, turn **left** after 700 meters at **Hollow Mountain Road**. This packed dirt road, the lowest crossing over the North Mountains, is only 7 km long, and its condition is usually adequate for most bikes. A few gentle climbs and the tour's worst road is over and you come out on **Shore Road**.

The difference in weather between the valley and the shore is startling. On the shore, where the Bay of Fundy influences the weather, it can be cool and foggy; in the valley, where the North Mountains and South Hills shelter the valley from the moist winds, the climate can be bright and warm.

Emerging on paved Shore Road, to your left 1 km is Delaps Cove, where a 3-km trail leads to a 13-meter-high waterfall. As you return to the junction with Hollow Mountain Road, the road now rolls (sometimes steeply) beside the Bay of Fundy's shore. During the next 8.5 km of riding, the route offers expansive views up the bay, as you pass by the quiet town of **Hillsburn** and the scenic fishing settlement of **Parkers Cove**. The road continues, and you are now on one of the lines of the "Underground Railway."

Before the American Civil War, fugitive slaves escaped from the United States—with the help of a loose network of abolitionists—and reached freedom in Nova Scotia. Some settled along the Fundy coast, persevering against the harsh conditions along the Bay of Fundy and subsequent discrimination of the Nova Scotians. Some stone walls and foundations remain—memorials to the spirit and dignity that remained of an enslaved race.

Beyond Parkers Cove 600 meters is Parker Mountain Road, which is the first paved road crossing the North Mountains from Annapolis Royal 9 km away. For the next 14 km stay on **Shore Road**, which continues to roll within the bay's sight.

Be careful of the steep downhill 14.5 km from Parker Mountain Road as you approach **Hampton**. The road ascends to Hampton 300 meters farther. Cycling 2 km past Hampton, turn **right** at **Hampton Mountain Road** to begin the ascent up the windward face of the North Mountains. This road's ascent feels confusing. It climbs and then seemingly dips, but it always feels as if you're climbing. You even have to engage in a battle of wits with Magnetic Hill. After passing a CAUTION sign, continue past Arlington Road, and stop beside the sixth utility pole (sometimes marked in red). Once you have stopped pedaling, the magnetic attraction will draw your bike backward up the hill. It's no wonder this climb feels painfully difficult; you also have to grapple with magnetic forces! About 4 km from the Shore Road you reach the top of the pass. Don't stop now though, because in another km you reach **Valleyview Provincial Park** with its picnic area, campground, and omniscient view over the Annapolis Valley.

Valleyview Provincial Park to Kentville: 90 kilometers

From the Valleyview Lookoff you gaze down into a valley that stretches for 160 km from Digby to Windsor. Its width ranges from 8 to 24 km. Protected from extreme weather by the basalt ridge you are standing on, the Annapolis Valley, carved for millennia by glaciers and rivers, has become one of the world's most famous apple-growing regions. The view over the patchwork farmlands, small villages, and forested South Hills is from a throne-like perch.

Dropping from the steep descent, make sure you adjust your brakes, inflate your tires, and strap your panniers on tightly. The downhill ends quickly although you can reach speeds of 70 kph easily. After 5 quick km you reach the intersection of **Church Street** and **Granville Street** in **Bridgetown**.

From the corner of Church and Granville turn **right** on **Granville Street**, and after 100 meters turn **left** on **Queen Street**. Cycling along Queen, cross over the Annapolis River, and after 1.5 km, you come to a T junction. Turn **left** following **201 East**, and 8 km later pass the junction to **Paradise**. As you cycle along quiet, pastoral 201 you can view the North Mountain ridge to your left, far enough to add grandeur, while to your right lay the South Hills, close enough to add gentle climbs to your pedaling. Remember that few provisions are available along this route. About 5 km past the junction to Paradise, over hilly terrain, is the junction to **Lawrencetown**, 2 km to the left. Continuing along 201 East, the route becomes more hilly but flattens after about 5 km past the Lawrencetown junction. Quietly, as most of the traffic has been siphoned off onto Highway 101 and the bustling, midtown Highway 1, you pass apple orchards and dairy farms. The views over the valley just become better, and after 11 km, you reach the intersection for **Highway 10**. To the south lies Lunenburg, 128 km away, and to the north is Middleton, 3 km away. A convenience store sits on the corner if you don't want to detour to Middleton for supplies.

Back on 201, after 6.5 km you reach another T intersection. Stay **left** toward Greenwood. **Highway 201** becomes level, but the traffic intensifies as you reach the junction for **Kingston** after 4 km, and the Greenwood shopping strip immediately beyond it. Beyond the intersection for Kingston 600 meters, bear **right** at the next intersection, continuing on **201 East**. You pass Canada's largest antisubmarine base, built for the Royal Canadian Air Force in 1942. Today the military uses it as a training base and maintains a search and rescue unit. Past **Greenwood**, after the final mall, the traffic disappears and the road continues past marshes and through forests. In another 8 km you arrive at **Highway 1**. Turn **right** along **1 East**. After 3 km you arrive in **Auburn**. To your left notice whitewashed St. Mary's Anglican Church, skillfully built by master carpenters and builders in the late 1700s. The parish built the church for Bishop Charles Ingles, who was an important catalyst during the Loyalist migration. Beyond Auburn 3 km, you come to **Aylesford** and **Victoria Road**. To your right 3 km is Oak Lawn Farm Zoo, exhibiting mammals, primates, cats, and birds. Turn **left** on **Victoria Road** toward the North Mountains. After 1 km, pass over Highway 101, and after another 1.2 km, passing apple orchards, turn **right** on **221 East**. This is the finest riding of the tour. Beside you, the face of the North Mountains rises abruptly, and as you cycle quietly on the mountain's flank you can admire the undulating valley while you cross pear and apple orchards, dairy and cattle farms. If you are in the area in late May, the apple trees will be exploding in white blossoms; if you are here in late September, the apple picking season will be well under way. After 18 km, you pass **Woodville General Store**, where the folktales flow like apple cider during the fall Harvest Festival. After another 4.5 km you pass another general store at **Kinsmen Corner**, and after another km, the **Lakeville General Store** marks the last of the small hamlets. Beyond the general store 300 km, you pass **Silver Lake** and turn **right** on **Lakewood Road**. The next major road you reach is **Highway 359**, 7 km farther. Turn **right** toward **Kentville**. Highway 359 is more hilly and has more traffic than quiet, level Lakewood Road. After 3 km along what the locals call **Cornwallis Street** you come to the junction to Highway 341, the route to Blomidon Peninsula. A km beyond this junction you come to Belcher Street, which you can use if you want to avoid Kentville and Highway 1. Past this intersection 400 meters you arrive at **Main Street**, the center of **Kentville**.

Kentville to Windsor: 42 kilometers

Kentville, the largest community in the valley, processes most of the region's apples. John Martin planted the valley's first apple in 1633, and today farmers still introduce new varieties of apples and other fruit. Blair House, in Kentville, is an on-site museum exhibiting everything you want to know about apples. Another site of interest in Kentville is the Kings County Courthouse, the seat of justice from 1903 to 1980, housing a collection of social and natural history artifacts. A final attraction is the Agriculture Canada Research Station where, with prior approval, you can take a guided tour over the extensive grounds.

From Main and Cornwallis streets the next section of the road is the messiest of the tour. Traffic builds and you have to pass intensive commercial activity. About 2 km from Main and Cornwallis streets you pass the turn for Highway 12, leading to New Ross Farm and Chester Basin on the Atlantic coast. About 3 km past Kentville, you pass through the center of **New Minas**, another business hub. After 6 km in the midst of activity, you reach a turn for Highway 358, leading to Blomidon Peninsula, and finally, after another 2 km, you reach **Wolfville**.

Wolfville, the second incorporated town in Canada, began its history as Mud Creek, but the townsfolk had to find a more dignified name when a judge's daughter became too embarrassed to tell others where she was from. As you bicycle into town notice the stately Victorian homes lining the road until you reach Wolfville's center, Acadia University's campus. Beyond the campus is the tourist office, which distributes pamphlets describing two excellent walking tours.

Past Wolfville 5 km you come to the turn for **Grand Pré**, 2 km to the **left**. The National Historic Site, Nova Scotia's second most visited tourist attraction, is a solemn place. To many visitors, and especially for the descendants of the expelled Acadians visiting from New Brunswick, Quebec, New England, and Louisiana, Grand Pré is a site of reverence and a symbol of their culture. It was here that one of Canada's most tragic events unfolded.

War broke out between England and France again in 1702, and Acadia became an easy target for New Englanders who repeatedly attacked and looted the settlements. The Treaty of Utrecht in 1713 ceded the peninsula of Nova Scotia to the English, but then the English minority had to govern the French majority. The English conditionally forced the Acadians to swear allegiance to the English—which was customary whenever a new monarch took the throne—but the Acadians claimed neutrality until both sides agreed to conditions granting the Acadians the right to practice Catholicism and to continue their ties with the Micmacs. The Acadians knew how important neutrality was, but the French viewed them as poor allies and the English viewed them as poor

The reconstructed interior courtyard at Port Royal National Historic Site

citizens. The envelope of the Acadians' fate was starting to seal. As incidents between the Micmacs and the English increased, the English governor, Charles Lawrence, became more worried about the Acadians, and in 1749 he demanded they swear an unconditional oath of allegiance. When the situation became more tense, he rejected Acadian neutrality. On July 28, 1755, he demanded their deportation. The Acadians' destiny was now in the hands of 2,000 hostile, anti-Catholic, New England recruits. The evacuation was ruthless. The ragged collection of troops burned houses, barns, and crops. Within hours they reduced a century's work to smoldering ruins. The subsequent expulsion obliterated Acadian society, shredding communities and families. The English expelled 12,000 Acadians to areas where they would be impotent. Due to storms and food shortages, one-third died en route, and with no support at landing areas, another third died after arriving. The Acadians had almost been exterminated. It wasn't until 1764 that the English allowed the Acadians to return. When they did, they found their homelands overtaken by the ubiquitous New Englanders. These dis-placed Acadians were forced to settle in inhospitable areas throughout the Maritimes. Today, the expulsion is the event that solidifies the Acadian culture.

The memorial site at Grand Pré shelters a stone church and an exhibit outlining the deportation. On the grounds is a re-creation of a blacksmith's shop, a formal garden, and a statue of Evangeline, the heroine of Henry Longfellow's epic poem documenting the event.

From Grand Pré the route becomes more tricky. In 1.5 km you merge onto **Highway 101 East**, but this busy route is necessary only because the bridge over Highway 1 collapsed. Highway 101 is not as fearsome as it sounds, as it is divided, has a wide shoulder, and your time on it is short. Just 0.5 km later exit on **Exit 9** and follow **Highway 1**, known as Grand Pré Road. This highway parallels 101 and is quieter and hillier. After 8 km, you come to the turn for **Hantsport**. You could continue straight, but it's no shorter than the tour and Hantsport is worth bicy-cling through. So turn **left**. After 1 km, you're in the small community, and after another 500 meters, you pass by the Hantsport Community Centre and Memorial Museum, containing marine memorabilia and models. Beyond the center 100 meters, you come to the intersection for **Highway 1**, where you turn left, staying on Highway 1. The road past Hantsport levels out and you ride along, merrily overlooking the reddish-brown Avon River. For the next 11 km you cross two sets of railway tracks (be careful) until you arrive in **Windsor**. Heading up Ferry Hill behind you is Gerish Street. On it is the Shand House, worth visiting to admire the cycling trophies in the drawing room and the 1890s photographs in the attic tower of the Halifax Cycling Club. Back in town on King Street, you can also see Fort Edward National Historic Site, which is the last surviving blockhouse in Nova Scotia. Originally part of Fort Edward, it was another Acadian deportation point, and today it is the oldest original structure in Canada.

The tour ends in Windsor. From here, you can continue along High-way 1 to Halifax, or cross Hants County to Truro, or take Highway 14 to Chester on the Atlantic coast.

TOUR NO. 5

GHOSTS, FOSSILS, AND BLUEBERRIES

Start / Finish: Amherst/Amherst
Distance: 329 kilometers (201 miles)
Estimated time: 4 days
Terrain: Hilly
Map: Nova Scotia—The Doer's and Dreamer's Complete Map
Connecting tours: Tour No. 12
Connections: Trans-Canada Highway 104

This tour covers the most underrated area in Nova Scotia. Physically challenging, the route passes marshes, roller-coaster hills, and isolated stretches of up to 40 km. Cycling, you might find the tour isolated, but the area has attracted a breed of people who have enjoyed the isolation and have flourished, despite the tragedies that have befallen them. Springhill, whose name was synonymous with catastrophe, has moved forward and fortified its spirit.

As you pass the shores of the Bay of Fundy, consider that its natural history stretches back from 300 million years ago, when the area was tropical forest, to the past century, when the area around Parrsboro prospered as a shipbuilding center. This tour offers solitude, beauty, and fulfillment. Few other areas in Nova Scotia combine these characteristics, making this trip one of the most worthwhile tours in the Maritimes. The isolated stretches from Amherst to Parrsboro and from Springhill to Wallace require that you maintain your supplies. Traffic is generally quiet, though it may pick up along Highway 366 between Pugwash and Amherst. You will be unable to find food or water for 40-km stretches, and the only bike shop is in Amherst.

Amherst to Advocate Harbour: 87 kilometers

The tour begins at the **Provincial Tourist Office**, a converted 1905 railway sleeping car. Pick up a Nova Scotia map and a pamphlet describing the town's historic landmarks. Amherst's history turns back to the Acadian era when it was the Maritimes' first town. In the early 1900s the town earned the nickname "Busy Amherst" because of the area's intensive manufacturing.

From the tourist office cycle 400 meters up **Lawrence Street** to **Victoria Street**. Turn **right**. After 300 meters, the road, now **Highway 6**, crosses over busy Trans-Canada 104. Continue straight and

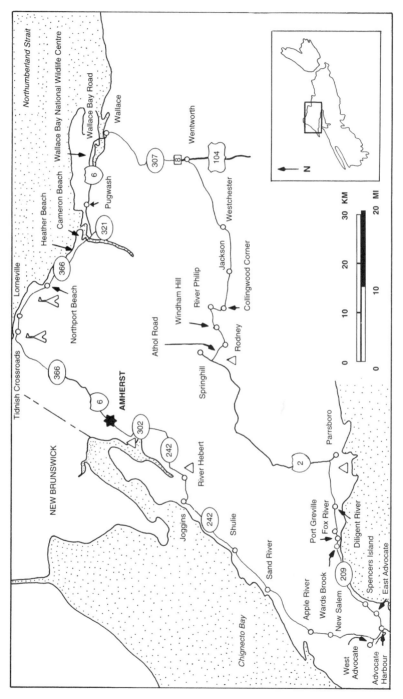

ride on the right next to the Amherst Point Migratory Bird Sanctuary.

Back on the tour, after 10 km past marsh and pastureland, veer **right** on **302**, and after about 1.5 km pass an experimental farm that offers guided tours. After about 2.7 km, take **242 right** toward River Hebert.

The next section of rolling hills continues for about 12.5 km until you reach **River Hebert**. This hamlet's main attraction is the Heritage Models Museum, which contains twenty-five miniature models of former and present buildings. The river the town is named after is an ideal spot from which to watch a natural phenomenon—the tidal bore. In certain v-shaped inlets around the Bay of Fundy, the voluminous tide enters as a broad ripple, but as the water is squeezed into the narrowing channel, the ripple grows into a wave, sometimes a meter high. The event's exact time and size vary with the weather, so arrive earlier than indicated in the calculated schedule that you can obtain at the Amherst Tourist Office.

From River Hebert, the road becomes slightly more rolling until **Joggins**, 5.5 km farther. Stock up on supplies here because the next section to Advocate Harbour is virtually deserted. Past the town's information booth 300 meters, you reach an intersection heading to Joggins' famous fossil cliffs.

Today visitors may keep any fossils they find on the beach that they can carry out but may not disturb anything in the cliffs. Signs near the cliffs also warn to be careful of rock slides and the bay's tides.

Continuing the tour, follow **Highway 242** to the **left**. The most isolated section of the tour begins as you leave Joggins. Cycling along the shore, it's hard to imagine busy shipbuilding towns once lined this coast. Along this route you can admire the views over Chignecto Bay. The road winds around and over the shore and becomes increasingly hilly. Each turn and sweep of the road offers a change of scene. A few km to the left is the Chignecto Game Sanctuary, which maintains a healthy population of moose, deer, and bear. Most of the animals roam at dusk and during the night, but you could still see some of the large mammals. Past Joggins 16 km you pass **Shulie**. Although the town offers no provisions, it does provide great views over the bay. Between Shulie and Sand River you climb and cross over the Tompkin Plain. The plain is slightly rolling and deserted. From Shulie 11 km, cross the bridge for **Sand River**. From Sand River the challenging road turns inland away from Chignecto Bay and toward **Apple River**, 12 km farther. The bridges along this section are narrow, so use caution. Past **Apple River Bridge** 2 km, you come to a T intersection. Turn **left** for Advocate. The other road leads to West Apple River, the first noticeably populated settlement since Joggins. A km farther continue **left** at the next T junction. The road's next section to **New Salem**, 4 km away, is relatively level. Beyond New Salem the road continues with steeper, shorter hills. After 9 km, shooting through a small gap in the hills, you arrive at the junction for **West Advocate**. This village offers the first accommodations and provisions since Joggins. Beyond West Advocate, you start viewing Advocate Bay and Cape d'Or and 2 km later you arrive in **Advocate Harbour**, providing provisions and accommodations.

Advocate Harbour to Parrsboro: 39.5 kilometers

Between Advocate Harbour and Parrsboro, places to buy provisions are sporadic. About 3 km from Advocate Harbour lies the junction to Cape d'Or, a spectacular cliff that drops into the Minas Channel. The road to the cape's end crosses over two steep, long hills, and in 5 km it ends at a lighthouse high on a ledge above the water.

Back on the main road, after passing **East Advocate**, the road becomes more hilly as it rises and drops into the small coves. Across Greville Bay you can see Cape Split, over 200 km away by road. After 5.5 km, you reach **Spencers Island**.

From Spencers Island the tour's most difficult section begins. The road oscillates along the shore, in places climbing to 100 meters and then dropping to sea level. Behind you are great views of Spencers Island and Cape d'Or. After cycling 16 km, you pass **Wards Brook** (no provisions) and 1 km later you come to a Y intersection. Continue **right** on **209**. Just 0.5 km later you reach **Port Greville** and a convenience store. Past **Fox River** 2 km, the road begins to flatten. After 7 km you pass **Diligent River**, crossing level to slightly rolling terrain. In another 10 km, you reach the junction to **Highway 2**. To your right is **Parrsboro**, 2.5 km away.

Parrsboro, the largest town in the Minas Basin, will look like a metropolis after the ride from Amherst. Historically, Parrsboro is one of the oldest continually inhabited regions in North America. Its position at the foot of the Cobequid Highlands pass and its natural harbor made the route important ever since the Micmacs camped in the area.

In the spring these First Peoples descended from their familial camps and gathered along the coast. They would celebrate with a massive clam bake, catch up on stories, feast, and revel at the survival of another severe winter. The Micmacs had no governing authority like that of the Blackfoot and Algonquin farther inland. During the summer, the men hunted and fished and the women farmed. In the winter, they would break into family groups and travel inland to hunt for game. They followed this yearly cycle for generations until the Europeans' first arrival in 1498 permanently transformed Micmac culture. The Micmacs then became more reliant on European trade goods and spent more time inland, concentrating on hunting and trapping. When winter came, the Micmacs neglected accumulating provisions for the winter and had to rely on the Europeans' dried goods. The spiral of dependency distanced the Micmacs from their traditional life, and they became pawns in the French struggle for North America.

The French used the Micmacs' unhappiness with the English—who refused to give presents as signs of diplomacy—to persuade them to conduct raids and massacres of the English. The French Acadians had always treated the Micmacs with respect, but the newly arrived English Loyalists, who claimed most of the land in Nova Scotia, refused to grant compensation to the Micmacs. Eventually, the provincial government gave land to the First People, but the lack of official surveying allowed the squatters to move in and overwhelm the

A sign for one of the many cheese farms around the Parrsboro area

Micmac territory. By 1860 the Micmacs retained only 8,000 hectares of a land they once revered.

Parrsboro prospered as a shipbuilding center. In the 1870s, 30 million tons of goods passed through the town every year. It had 5 hotels, 36 stores, and 200 registered vessels (more than it does today). The town began its quick decline when the era of the wooden ship ended and the Springhill mines closed down. Recently another shocking blow came when the Trans-Canada Highway opened, rerouting most of the trans-provincial travel. Today, the town depends on tourism, and it remains a headquarters for gem seekers who come to the basin looking for semiprecious stones such as agates and amethysts. The Fundy Geological Museum, one of Nova Scotia's newest museums, holds a collection of gems and dinosaur fossils found in the area. You can also see some of the largest tides in the world at Parrsboro. High tides can reach four stories, sometimes rising 2 meters an hour.

Parrsboro to Wallace: 115 kilometers

Leave Parrsboro the same way you entered, along **Highway 2**. After 14 km you pass **Newville Lake Picnic Park**. The road is generally level with intermittent climbs. After 12.5 km, you pass the junction to Highway 302, a route that returns to Amherst. Continuing along 2, the road begins to roll through forests of maple trees.

After about 19 km, closing in on Springhill, you come to **Black River Road**, which leads to **Springhill Miners' Museum**, 100 meters to the **right**. The museum is a living testament to Springhill's coal miners. Retired miners, who once worked in the Syndicate Mine, now display the miners' equipment and describe their daily routine. These proud men take visitors into the bowels of the mine and summarize the lives and echo the tragedies of the miners and their families. When the guide turns off all the lights in the shaft, the blackness is claustrophobic. You have only your imagination, slipping on the edge of panic. Black fear creeps into the shaft and your guts until the lights come on again. If you have never been in a mine, go.

Back along Highway 2, you have only to pedal another 2 km to arrive in **Springhill**.

The Anne Murray Centre sits on Springhill's main street. The new building is an interpretive center honoring Canada's most famous female vocalist. Resupply your provisions in town because, except for Collingwood, you will be unable to find food until Westchester, 55 km away. Retrace your route along **Highway 2** for 2 km, then turn **left** at **Athol Road**, heading to **Rodney** and **Windham Hill**. This quiet road pitches and rolls along the shoulder of the Cobequid Highlands. After about 15.5 km, you pass through **River Philip**. The road jogs **right**, and after another 2.5 km, turn **left** at **Collingwood Corner** toward **Jackson**. Collingwood Corner has the only convenience store along this road. Beyond this village the route becomes less hilly as you follow the River Philip Valley and enter Canada's wild blueberry capital.

About 25 km from Collingwood you arrive in **Westchester** and continue straight for another 12 km until you reach **Trans-Canada Highway 104**. Carefully turn **left** and stay on the wide, paved shoulder only for about a km to **Exit 8**, then turn **right** at **Wentworth**. Follow **307** along fairly level terrain until you come to a Y intersection. Stay on 307. After another 11 km, past pig farms, woods, and pasture, you arrive in **Wallace**.

Wallace to Amherst: 87.5 kilometers

Wallace's mainstays are fishing and sandstone mining. The parliamentary buildings in Canada's capital, Ottawa, were constructed from the henna-colored stones dug from the area. The town also produced a famous luminary: Simon Newcomb, a leading scientist and astronomer. From 1877 to 1897, Newcomb was the director of the *American Nautical Almanac*. His work allowed for the accurate prediction of the planets' orbits and lunar tables, which the world's observatories universally adopted. Near the Wallace Bay Bridge a plaque honors his memory.

From the corner of Highway 307 and Highway 6 turn **left** on **Highway 6**. Traffic can be intense along this highway, but you have to follow it for only about a km before you turn **right** on **Trunk 6**. Cross the bridge over the marshes in Wallace Bay, and after 2 km turn **left** on **Wallace Bay Road**. After 6 km, you enter the **Wallace Bay National Wildlife Centre**. During the migratory seasons of spring and fall, the area is alive with hundreds of types of birds. After 7 km turn **right** back onto **Highway 6** toward Pugwash. This short section of 6 has moderate traffic but impressive views over the Cobequid Hills behind you. Another 5 km bring you to **Pugwash**.

Pugwash, one of the more unusual names in Nova Scotia, derives from the Micmac word *pagweak*, meaning "shallow water of the shoal." Today, the busy harbor accommodates cargo ships carrying lumber cut from the Cobequid forests and thousands of tons of salt from the nearby salt mine. A jumble of ropes tether the bright blue and red fishing boats. Tourist crafts, bedecked with deck chairs and coolers, sail into the harbor to visit the town and shop at the famous pewter shops.

Turn **left**, staying on Highway 6 for 7 km, until you reach **Highway 321**, where you turn **right**, staying on Highway 6. After another 1.5 km you pass **Chase Lobster Pond**, a processing plant for the lobsters caught in Northumberland Strait. You can drop in for a look. As you travel past the small harbors along this next section, you might be lucky enough to watch the lobster boats returning from trapping. The fishing crews chug off at first light and return with the day's lobster catch in the early afternoon. Some of the crews will sell you a lobster right off the boat. From the pond it is a little over 1 km until you turn **right** on **Highway 366**. The road through this section is flat to slightly rolling, and for the next 17.5 km you pass dairy farms and the small cottage communities of **Heather Beach**, **Cameron Beach**, and **Northport Beach** (provincial park and public beach). The beaches along the Northumberland Strait offer some of the Maritimes' warmest water. After 7 km, you pass **Lorneville**, and after another 4.5 km, you come to **Tidnish Crossroads**, marked by a convenience store. The Tidnish Dock Provincial Park lies 500 meters to the right.

In the 1890s the fiasco of the Tidnish Railway brought the cost of confederation into painful focus for the region's people. Henry Ketchum, entrepreneur and renegade railroad baron, had just finished his railroad-building in Brazil and conceived the idea of building a railroad line to transport 50-ton schooners 27 km overland between Tidnish and Fundy Bay. This section of railroad promised to bring

back the age of sail. Ships would save 1,040 km and bypass the dangerous waters around Nova Scotia. The forsaken coastal towns, left
behind by steamships, ached for the return of their glory days and desperately wanted the line. European bankers and the federal and local
governments backed the ambitious project and granted Ketchum funds
and the needed land. After his success in Brazil anything seemed possible. Ketchum's plans were extravagant. He brought in 4,000 workers
from Italy, built a church for the area, and imported ready-cut stones
from Scotland. As work began on the railway, costs skyrocketed. The
deep marshes hampered the railbed, and the engineers had underesti-
mated the Fundy tides. But the loans kept coming. Ketchum had com-
pleted the hydraulic lifts and 19 km of track when money ran out for
the last time. Europe had entered a recession, and a new Canadian
government, wanting to distance itself from the old administration and
hamper old political allies, refused its support. The government, centered in Ontario and Quebec, pushed its agenda to the forefront. Confederation had rejected the people of the Maritimes and their dreams.
Ketchum's dream became a colossal waste. He lived the rest of his life
bankrupt, broken, and bitter. His last request was to be buried near
his unfinished railway. In the park you can see bits of masonry and
part of the railbed, token reminders of a costly, grandiose dream.

   Back on 366, after 4 km of level country, **cross** the Tidnish River. If
you look to your left, you can see a culvert, a remnant of the Tidnish
Railway. Just beyond the bridge is a turn for the ferry to Prince
Edward Island at Port Elgin. Passing through quiet farmland, after 19
km turn **right** on **Highway 6**. As you finish the tour and begin entering the Amherst area, you pass by the Trantamar marshes. These
marshlands, called the "world's largest hayfield," are the most produc-
tive ecosystems found anywhere. The grasses and mud flats of the
marshes provide food for fish, shellfish, and hundreds of species of
birds. For example, one shrimp-like crustacean, the *corophium*, may
number as many as 70,000 per square meter of mud surface. The tides
carry the organic material of the marshes out to sea, providing nutri-
ents for the fisheries. Today, Ducks Unlimited and the Nova Scotia
government manage the area.

   After 4 km, turn **right** on **Victoria Street**, and 400 meters later,
you arrive back at **Amherst's tourist office**.

TOUR NO. 6

CAPE GEORGE

Start/Finish: Antigonish/Antigonish
Distance: 63.3 kilometers (39.5 miles)
Estimated time: 1 day
Terrain: Very hilly
Map: Nova Scotia—The Doer's and Dreamer's Complete Map
Connecting tours: None within a day's bicycling
Connections: Trans-Canada Highways 104 and 103

The clash of sea and the Pictou-Antigonish Highlands created the 190-meter highland of Cape George. The steep hills begin after a brief pastoral scene of cattle and creeks. Along the high escarpment you can enjoy views over Prince Edward Island and Cape Breton. The road skims past the fishing village of Ballantynes Cove then rolls over gentler hills, passing by lakes, salt marshes, and beaches, finally arriving back in Antigonish.

Antigonish has supermarkets. Malignant Cove and Ballantynes Cove have convenience stores. **Potable water is difficult to find on this tour due to the contamination of the ground wells**. You must rely on Antigonish for tap water or convenience stores along the route for bottled water. The only bike shop is in Antigonish.

Finally, southwest winds can increase over Northumberland Strait during the day. Start early for calmer weather.

Antigonish to Antigonish: 77.3 kilometers

The name Antigonish comes from the Micmac word meaning "the place where branches were broken off trees by bears gathering beechnuts." Thank the Micmac for brevity. You begin the tour at the corners of **Hawthorne and Main streets**. Up to your left, over the bridge, is the campus of St. Francis-Xavier University. The 2,300 students who attend the university are one of the town's economic mainstays.

At the corner of Hawthorne and Main, turn **right** on **245 West**, and after 2 km, you leave the town limits. Out on the open road the kilometers roll gently through pastureland populated by unperturbed cows and idyllic streams. About 21 km from Antigonish, you reach the junction with Highway 337. Beyond the junction 50 meters, on 245 West, is a small general store. Stock up here since no provisions are available until you're back in Antigonish. Turn **right** on **337**. Your first views

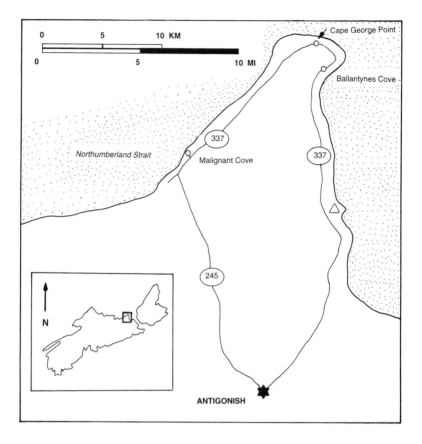

over the Northumberland Strait pop into view as the road begins its roller-coaster ride to Cape George.

About 4 km beyond the intersection is the junction for Malignant Cove, 2 km to the left. Although it's the most repugnant name in Nova Scotia, Malignant Cove's name originated from the wreck of the HMS *Malignant*.

Once you reach **Cape George Point** you can exult in the extensive view of headlands, churning sea, and Cape Breton. Cape George is Northumberland Strait's most prominent landmark. Originally, the French called it Cap St. Louis. After a number of wrecks, including the *Malignant*, the first lighthouse was built in 1861.

After another 5 km, passing through hilly terrain and forests alternating with pastureland, you begin the drop into **Ballantynes Cove**. Before you descend, drink in the view below: St. Georges Bay, the wharves that protect the small fishing fleet, the village, and the red cliffs.

Beyond Ballantynes Cove the road rolls through pastureland and

Cormorants nest on old bridge pilings near Antigonish.

weaves between small creeks, lakes, and marshes. About 17 km beyond town a junction to the left goes to **Crystal Cliffs**, where pink gypsum bluffs rise out of the blue waters. Another 17 km take you back to **Main Street**. After 1 last km of city riding, you arrive at the starting point—the intersection of **Hawthorne and Main streets**.

TOUR NO. 7

THE CABOT TRAIL

Start/Finish: Baddeck/Baddeck
Distance: 293.5 kilometers (179 miles)
Estimated time: 3 to 4 days or more
Terrain: Mountainous
Maps: Cape Breton Tourist Map (Department of Tourism), plus individual park maps (available at park entrances)
Connecting tours: Tour No. 8
Connections: Trans-Canada Highway 105; Highway 19; North Sydney ferries to Port aux Basques and Argentia, Newfoundland

The Cabot Trail, the classic Maritimes ride, attracts cyclists worldwide for a number of reasons. The first and most important is the scenery: from the wide plateaus of the Margaree River to the wild uplands of the Highland Mountains, the Cabot Trail offers scenery that will stop you in mid-pedal stroke. The trail presents the challenge of leg-searing ascents and brake-searing, hairpin corners. Every year, from May to September, approximately 4,000 cyclists set out to conquer it.

The cold Labrador current influences the area, making Cape Breton the province's coolest area. Most of the rain falls in spring and fall, but even in early May and late September snow flurries are still possible. The spring winds on the trail can be brutal; on the trail's gulf side even the trees grow on a slant. As the cycling season progresses, the winds decrease until September. The prevailing winds gust from the west, but because the land's contours funnel and bend the wind into endless directions, it may always feel as if you are cycling against a headwind. The forest on the Atlantic acts as a shield from the wind.

Realistically, you can travel this tour from the middle of May to late September. Spring, the season of regeneration and overflowing streams, produces the strongest winds. From late June to Labour Day (the first weekend in September), tourists in the tens of thousands descend on the area and you have to start competing for accommodations and the locals' civility. Summer is also the season of the weakest winds. In autumn, most of the pests, insect and otherwise, have left for warmer climates and you can enjoy the spectacle of the green maple and birch leaves changing to red, brown, and gold.

Scenery is not the only draw to Cape Breton. Ever since the native Micmacs, someone has traveled through the area. The Portuguese,

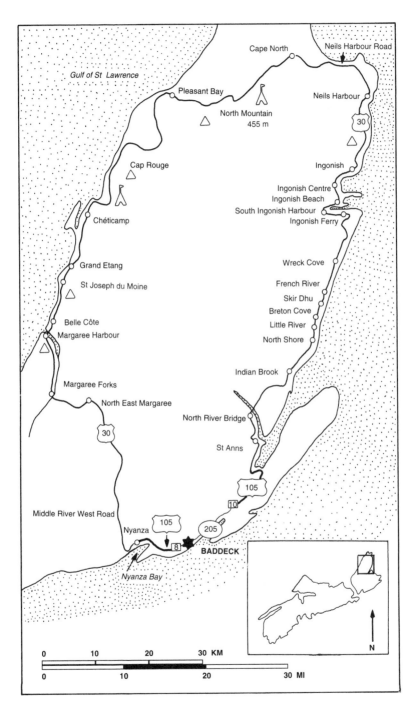

French, English, and Scottish all settled on the island, but it is the French and Scottish who maintain a cultural presence. Visit the Acadian Museum in Chéticamp to watch rug hooking and enjoy a traditional Acadian meal. Alternatively, Lone Sheiling, outside Pleasant Bay, is a re-creation of a lone shepherd's hut modeled after a crofter's cottage on the Isle of Skye.

From Baddeck you cycle a short distance along the Trans-Canada Highway. You traverse the island through the Middle and Margaree river valleys, finally emerging at the Gulf of St. Lawrence. The first day ends at Chéticamp, a bastion of Acadian culture. Just beyond the town you enter Cape Breton Highlands National Park, where you cross forested mountains laced with waterfalls, stream-threaded valleys, and lonely plateaus of bogs and barrens. The route chugs over the mountains as you attack the long ascents. You rise and fall from sea level, reaching as high as 450 meters. The tour's second day ends at a primitive campground near the park boundaries. You could bicycle from Chéticamp to Ingonish in one day, but it would be exhausting. If you don't want to camp, you can stay at either Pleasant Bay or Cape North. Try not to rush though the tour; you should cherish it. From Cape North the route detours off the trail to Whites Point and Neils Harbour, eventually arriving at Ingonish. This supply spot for the trail's western side is a good spot to rest before the final day's ascent of Cape Smokey and the level ride back to Baddeck. Keep well supplied. No supplies are available within the park. Outside the park areas, basic facilities are available. The only bike shops are off the route at Sydney and Glace Bay. Ensure you tune your bike, particularly the brakes. The route does not have bike shops or repairs. On the trail maintain your brakes, cables, brake pads, and all your bolts. Check your bike and equipment before starting a day's ride. A final word of caution: Don't hang anything off your bike that may fall into your wheels or chain.

Only a few communities dot the route so local traffic is low. Tourist traffic, however, is intense. Nova Scotia's tourist department estimates that half a million people travel around the trail yearly. The hectic bus and tourist traffic peaks between July and August. Generally, the trail's roads have no shoulder, so the earlier you start in the day the better, as the daily traffic is most intense in the early afternoon.

Baddeck to Chéticamp: 93 kilometers

Baddeck is a yachting resort, a town of about 950, that provides full services to help prepare you for the tour's first stage. Kilometer 0 is the Alexander Graham Bell National Historic Park.

Start by heading **west** along **Highway 205**. After about 3 km, merge with **Trans-Canada Highway 105—Exit 8**. The highway might be busy, but it has a paved shoulder and is fine for cycling. After 8 km of slightly rolling terrain, you come to the beginning of the Cabot Trail. Continue straight so you can miss any busy traffic, and before merging with the Cabot Trail, you'll cycle along one of the region's prettier valleys. For the next 4 km ride beside Nyanza Bay.

After you pass the settlement of **Nyanza**, cross the bridge over Middle River. Then turn **right** on **Middle River West Road**. This secondary road immediately starts climbing and passing spruce and birch forest. Beyond the hills, when the land begins to open, houses and farms dot the roadside. After a little over 9.5 km, you come to a junction heading to Middle River. Keep **left** following the west shore. After another 9 km, passing the junction to Upper Middle River, you come to a junction.

You are now on the **Cabot Trail**, officially Highway 30. Although the traffic increases, the road is safe. You reach the highest point of this section (105 meters) after about 3 km, and then the road follows the peaceful shores of Lake O'Law, cradled by the Three Sisters Mountains. After about 8 km, you enter the Margaree River Valley Plateau. This wide plain hugs the Margaree, Baddeck, and Middle rivers. Scots from the Isle of Skye, led by "King Ross," first settled the area. Today, fishing people recognize it as one of Canada's most beautiful salmon rivers. Another 3 km from the junction to Margaree Valley you arrive in **North East Margaree**, containing the Margaree Salmon Museum, which reveals everything about the salmon fishing industry.

From North East Margaree the road heads west, winding its way to the Gulf of St. Lawrence. After a little over 8.5 km, passing by Mount Coady—named after M. M. Coady, founder of the Antigonish movement (which is the first cooperative in Atlantic Canada to help impoverished fishermen and farmers)—you come to **Margaree Forks**. Watch for hawks riding the thermal currents and looking for prey in the fields. Staying on the Cabot Trail and heading north through the Margaree River Valley, you descend to the Gulf of St. Lawrence. Past Margaree Forks 12 km, you come to the junctions of the South West and North West Margaree rivers and the Celidh (pronounced kay´-lee) and Cabot trails.

A couple of kilometers to your left is **Margaree Harbour** where you can visit the *Marion Elizabeth*, a fishing schooner built in 1918 in Lunenburg. Initially, fishing crews used the ship to harvest cod off Newfoundland, then rum runners used it for smuggling liquor during Prohibition, and today it is a floating museum/restaurant. You also can board a charter boat to take you to Margaree Island to visit the seabird colonies.

Turning **right**, continuing along the **Cabot Trail**, you cross one of the longest wooden bridges east of Montreal. The terrain changes from the interior's hilly forests to the coastal meadows and windswept slopes. The land looks sparse. The wind and salt spray have stunted the trees. The pounding surf crashes into the open bluffs. You enter a new section of the trail physically and culturally.

The Margaree River borders an area of Acadian culture. Along this coast this distinct group still speaks a seventeenth-century French dialect that even surprises French travelers. Everyone can still speak English, so don't worry about communicating with the locals. Passing **Belle Côte** the road rolls. After 7 km, you pass a lookout offering sweeping views over the Gulf of St. Lawrence and the southern part of the island. After another km you pass the Scarecrow Theatre, a

One of the scarecrows of the scary Scarecrow Theatre

creepy-looking side show boasting close to a hundred scarecrows dressed in weird clothing and poses. After 3 km you pass **St. Joseph du Moine**, and after another 3 km you pass **Grand Etang**. Yet another 10 km farther along this windswept plateau, you arrive at St. Peter's Church in **Chéticamp**.

Chéticamp to Big Intervale Campground: 54.5 kilometers

Chéticamp, a fishing and tourist village, supplies the Cabot Trail's western portion. Only 3,500 people live in town and you should stock up—you will find few supplies between here and Ingonish. The town's location is a harbinger of the terrain that awaits you. Sitting at the highland's foothills, Chéticamp will have you appreciating the future climbs. The walls of mountains beckon your imagination and put a tingle of anticipation in your legs.

The townspeople maintain a tenacious pride. Despite the tens of thousands of tourists who visit, the Acadians have managed to keep their culture alive. At the Chéticamp Acadian Museum you can watch demonstrations of wool carding, spinning, weaving, and rug hooking. The museum restaurant celebrates Acadian cuisine, including fried chicken, *rappie* (meat pie), and *poutine* (French fries with gravy and cheese curds).

Now that you are rested from yesterday's effort, your legs are refueled, and you are stocked up with food, the road leaves town and heads toward the highlands. After 6.5 km you reach the entrance to **Cape Breton Highlands National Park**. Stop at the Visitor's Centre to register, pay the fees if you plan to camp or use any trails, take a look at the exhibits, and learn more details of the park's habitats. If mountain biking interests you, find out which trails are open. If you did not stay overnight in Chéticamp, there's a campground next to the Visitor's Centre.

Leaving the area, the road slips into the puckered Bernard Valley and heads gently upward toward the Gulf of St. Lawrence. Pass the scree-covered slopes of Grand Falaise and the first small hill rises to greet you. Past the reception area 4 km you arrive at a 44-meter-high lookout. Continuing, you pass Le Bloque, foundations of the Acadian families' homes, abandoned when the park opened in 1936. As you start climbing the next hill, the magnitude of the trail hits you. Slinking beside the sea, undulating over the crests of the hills, and dipping invisibly into the cliffs, the silver trail of the road crosses some of the

An artisan at the Chéticamp Acadian Museum demonstrates rug-hooking.

most magnificent scenery east of the Rocky Mountains. You can see the next hour's cycling lying before you, and every twist, turn, and drop in the road offers you new breathtaking vistas.

The road's next section follows the shoreline's dramatic contours. From 0 to 100 meters above sea level, the road snakes along, affording lookouts and picnic areas where you can stop and admire the vistas. After about 4 km, at **Cap Rouge** (elevation 39 meters) you come to one of the most photographed sights in Nova Scotia. The Cabot Trail, looking like a river of mercury and ready to slip into the ocean on the slightest shake, climbs between the shore and highlands. After a little over 3 km, after passing another lookout and primitive campground, the road veers inland, following the steep sides of **Jumping Brook**. This, the first of three major climbs on the trail, crawls to the top of the plateau after 5.5 km. You are at the crest of French Mountain, a remote plain of scrub and brush, the tour's highest point and the highest paved road in Nova Scotia—459 meters. For the next 12 km the road rolls slightly (sneaking a couple of hills onto the route) over an area known as the Boarsback and weaves between bogs, ponds, hills, and lookouts spanning the chasms of the forest-covered precipices. After a small rise over Mackenzies Mountain, suddenly the road begins to plummet toward Pleasant Bay. For 4 km the road twists and turns on itself, spiraling in 10 to 12 percent grades, reaching the village nestled in the valley of the Grande Anse River. You can pick up basic foodstuffs in **Pleasant Bay**, and, if the weather is terrible, you can stay at the local motel just outside of town.

The French originally called the area Grande Anse; the succeeding English called it Limbo Bay, but it wasn't until 1819 that the area became inhabited. A nearby shipwreck stranded a small group of Scottish settlers on the bay's shore, and after spending a winter in the area they decided it was hospitable enough to stay and call it home. This small pocket of land remained isolated for the next hundred years. Living primarily on fishing and farming, the settlers traded with nearby Neils Harbour, settled by Newfoundlanders. Until 1927, visitors could reach the hamlet only by boat or on foot. In 1936 the Cabot Trail opened, but it was so narrow that drivers would have to call ahead to find out if they would meet any oncoming traffic. In 1962 the road was fully paved.

The road now heads inland, skirting the park's northern boundary. For the next 5 km, enjoy the flat terrain because the road, clinging to the cliff sides, begins to climb the narrow valley. About 6 km from Pleasant Bay you come to a trail that leads 800 meters to **Lone Sheiling**, a replica of the stone huts used by the crofters (Scottish shepherds) on Scotland's Isle of Skye. Continuing to ascend, you reach the crest of **North Mountain** (455 meters) after about 3.5 km. Stay on **Sammy's Barren** for about 4 km and then begin the quick, tricky descent along **MacGregor Brook** to **Sunrise Valley**. Stop at some of the lookouts, revel in their drama, and let your brakes and daring cool down.

At the park boundary and the bottom of the 3.5-km descent, lies **Big Intervale Campground**. The campsite is primitive so you have to bring all your equipment and boil the water you pull from the river. If you want more comfortable surroundings, Cape North beckons 11 km down the road.

Big Intervale Campground to Ingonish: 48.5 kilometers

From the campground the road slips down between the bluffs of the North Mountains for 11 km until it reaches **Cape North**. This small town offers basic services and acts as a junction for the road up to Meat Cove, Nova Scotia's most northern point. A local history museum is open during the tourist season. Continuing on the Cabot Trail, the road turns southeast and after about 4.5 km you turn **left** on **Neils Harbour Road**. This rolling route, about 5 km longer than the Cabot Trail, is a scenic detour passing spectacular white cliffs to Neils Harbour. After 9.5 km, you come to the junction to Whites Point, a modest settlement. Continue **right**. The first section is steep but then rolls down and inland, finally reaching the sea again. Veering inland 8.5 km and crossing the headland, you come to **Neils Harbour**, a picturesque town of white houses and a lighthouse. A km later you rejoin the Cabot Trail—turn **left**. After 5 km of rolling terrain, you pass **Black Brook**, and over one last rise you start rolling along a rocky, craggy coastline. This side of the trail is not as awesome as the gulf side, but it has more intimate beauty. As you roll along, you pass the landmarks: **Wreck Beach**, **Boiler Point**, **Shoal Point**, and **Red Head**. Sailors, from the Portuguese to the lobster fishing crews of today, have used these rocky promontories as navigation aids. Streams trickle into the sea as the swells become waves, pounding into cliffs. After about 9 km, the route leaves the park and enters the **Ingonish** pocket of development.

Ingonish to Baddeck: 97 kilometers

Through this area the settlements of **Ingonish**, **Ingonish Centre**, **Ingonish Beach**, **South Ingonish Harbour**, and **Ingonish Ferry** spread out along the trail over 16 km. Ingonish is also the supply town for the trail's Atlantic section. The Portuguese first settled in the area in 1521, but after they abandoned the fishing camp the French and the English moved in. The development now stretches for 7.5 km until you reenter the park, slip over the headland, and pass the world-class golf course and resort of Keltic Lodge. After 2 km you leave the park for the last time and the road circles **Ingonish Harbour**. You reach **Ingonish Ferry** after 7 km and begin the long slow ascent up Cape Smokey, climbing the valley of Red Head Brook and reaching the plateau after 6 km. At the top of the plateau from the lookout at Cape Smokey Provincial Park, you can enjoy extensive views out to sea.

The ecology of the area has been threatened seriously in the last decades. In 1968 a devastating fire, started by carelessness, charred the hillside forests. Since then the spruce budworm has ravaged the new trees.

The descent begins suddenly. After less than 3 km, you drop 366 meters down a road carved into the cliff side. Be careful at the bottom of the descent because the road switches back there. From the bottom of Cape Smokey, if you take a look back up the cliff side, the drop will send shivers up your spine. Then the road calms down. For the next 30 km you pass the tiny settlements of **Wreck Cove**, **French River**, **Skir Dhu**, **Breton Cove**, **Little River**, **North Shore**, and **Indian Brook**. These settlements, ranging in population from ten to thirty-eight, offer a few basic services, including the seasonal lobster sandwiches served from roadside kiosks. Following the rolling terrain, 3 km beyond Indian Brook you come to the junction of Highway 312. Stay on the **Cabot Trail**. The relatively flat road veers inland, following the Barachois River, squeezing through a smaller valley, and then opens up onto the South Brook Valley. After 9 km, you arrive at **North River Bridge**, another minuscule settlement. After another 9.5 km you come to **St. Anns**.

Past St. Anns 6 km you pass the Gaelic College of Celtic Arts, one of the world's last remaining centers of Gaelic culture. You can watch classes in bagpipes, clan lore, highland dancing, weaving, and Gaelic singing.

From 1815 to 1835, the promise of 40 hectares of free land lured the Scots to migrate to Nova Scotia, particularly to a land that was similar to their homeland. On Cape Breton they became boatbuilders and fishermen; others, enticed by the free land, went into the interior to try farming. Most of the farms failed because of the terrain and the difficulty of clearing the virgin forest.

Past the college 0.5 km, you reach **Trans-Canada Highway 105**. Turn **left** and start the last stretch back to Baddeck. This final section of road is wide, safe, and monotonous. After 8.5 km you come to the intersection with **Highway 205**. Exit at **Exit 10** and follow the road for 8 km into Baddeck.

TOUR NO. 8

LOUISBOURG

Start / Finish: Sydney/Sydney
Distance: 132.7 kilometers (81 miles)
Estimated time: 2 days
Terrain: Flat
Map: Cape Breton Island
Connecting tours: Tour No. 7
Connections: Trans-Canada Highway 125

The area around Sydney has long been renowned for coal. The French discovered the seams in the early 1700s; Cape Bretoners exploited it beginning in the 1850s, and ever since, coal has been the mainstay of the region's economy. Today tourists can find diamondlike attractions scattered among these old coal lands.

The route begins as you follow the rolling forests south of Sydney and the broad Mira River. After a half day of peaceful cycling you come to the historical gem of Nova Scotia and the largest historical re-creation in Canada, the Fortress of Louisbourg National Historic Park. Nestled in a far corner of Canada, this 6,700-hectare historic park was rebuilt with the same tools and diligence building it would have taken 250 years ago. This stunning re-creation becomes more authentic with the help of dozens of costumed guides who reenact the daily scenes that would have occurred when the fortress was in its heyday. Don't miss it.

The tour continues, passing sapphire waters and a coastline bejeweled with colorful ports. The climate is temperate inland, but wind can be a factor along the coast. Calculate at least two days to complete the tour, as you need to spend at least a half day at the fortress and you could be tempted by the beaches along the route.

Grocery stores are abundant on the route. However, the main centers for supplies are Sydney, Louisbourg, and Glace Bay, and the only bike shop is in Sydney. Traffic can be busy around the Sydney and Glace Bay areas and can be busy elsewhere on weekends.

Sydney to Fortress of Louisbourg National Historic Site: 50.6 kilometers

Despite Sydney's history of coal mining and iron smelting, it has a modern commercial feel. Since Sydney acts as Cape Breton's business hub, the town is bright and bustling. If you have the time you could visit St. George's Church, one of the oldest Anglican churches in

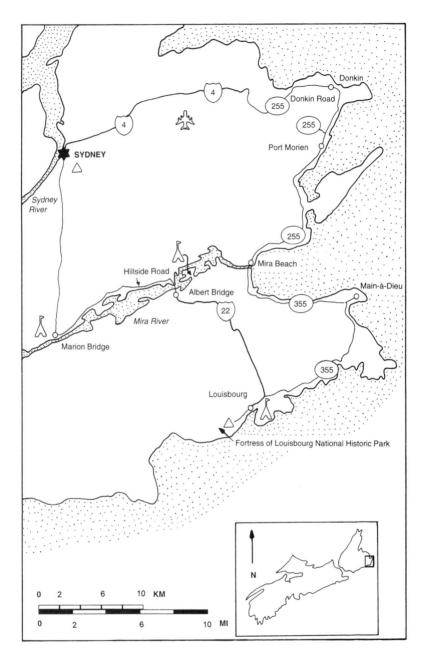

Fortress of Louisbourg National Historic Park

Canada, and St. Patrick's Cathedral, now a museum that documents the history of Cape Breton and Sydney.

From the corner of **Prince Street** and the **Esplanade**, where **Highway 4** turns at a right angle, head **south** following the Sydney River. Keep the mirrored City Hall to your right, and a km farther turn **left** on **Alexandra Street**, **Highway 327**. After 2 blocks, Alexandra veers to the **right**, and 2.7 km from Highway 4 you cross the overpass for

Two costumed "homesteaders" at the Fortress of Louisbourg

125 and leave the city. You follow a quiet, level road, dotted with ponds and hyphenated by small homes. In another 14 km you arrive at the town of **Marion Bridge**. Before the bridge in town, turn **left** on **Hillside Road**, hugging the broad Mira River.

You continue, following the banks of one of Nova Scotia's longest rivers, until you come to the junction with **22**, 13 km farther, where you turn **right**. A km farther on 22 you arrive at **Albert Bridge**. If you turn left for 2 km on Brickyard Road, you would come to Mira River Provincial Park, which offers camping and swimming. Back on 22, the terrain becomes slightly more hilly, and you can expect traffic to increase on weekends. Past Albert Bridge 17 km, you enter the town of **Louisbourg**. Watch for the tourist information booth and railway museum to your right. In another km you pass the center of town, which offers full provisions. Depending on the time you arrive, you can visit the park for the rest of the day or you can wait until morning. Plan to spend at least half a day. About 1.5 km from the town center, staying on the main road, turn **right**, following the signs for the park. In another 2 km you arrive at the entrance to **Fortress of Louisbourg National Historic Park**. An attendant will direct you to where you should leave your bike (usually near the Visitor Reception Centre). No bikes are allowed at the site. You pay the entrance fee at the Reception Centre, from where a shuttle bus takes all visitors to the fort's entrance.

Louisbourg to Sydney: 82.1 kilometers

The original fortress of Louisbourg lasted for only forty years, but its existence played a pivotal role in Canada's history. It was the guardian over the St. Lawrence River and, therefore, France's main waterway to Quebec. Louisbourg's history began in 1713. The previous European war had ended, and France had lost its ports in Newfoundland and the Bay of Fundy. All that remained of France's Maritime holdings were Cape Breton Island, then called Ile Royale, and Prince Edward Island, then called Ile St. Jean. Louisbourg was conceived and built to protect the Gulf of St. Lawrence. From its vantage point it could monitor and control movement in the gulf and provide a passageway for the French fur trade farther inland. Its strategic importance in the continental struggle was decisive.

Over the past thirty-five years, historians and park officials have reconstructed Louisbourg. Meticulously using the same tools and methods as the original inhabitants, the workers have reconstructed the fifty buildings stone by stone. The interiors are filled with a mixture of original and new furnishings. Look for the King's Governor's Quarters, the Soldiers' Barracks, the Fortress, and the Chapel.

The site encompasses 40 hectares, one-quarter of the original town's design. Within the town's walls, costumed interpreters, who for two

Opposite: Two costumed "guards" protect the entrance to the Fortress of Louisbourg.

years have studied the history and the original settlers' way of life, are ready to answer any questions. Throughout the town, the guides reenact scenes: a small impromptu auction takes place, a drunk soldier is dragged to the compound, and a group of costumed children dances to musicians' melodies. The historians have made every effort to maintain the site's historical integrity. If you imagine the site without tourists, you will feel as if you've slipped back in time.

Back on **Highway 22**, you return through the town of **Louisbourg**, and about 3 km farther, you turn right onto **355** (**Marconi Trail East**). This narrow road rolls past forest, lakes, and rock for 14 km to **Main-à-Dieu**. Ironically, the town's name was corrupted from the Micmac word *mandoo*, meaning "devil," to its French name meaning "hand of God." Today it looks more like the latter. This little port, sprinkled with bright blue, yellow, and white homes, hugs the entrance to Mira Bay. Beside the road, a series of boardwalks sprawls across the small dunes so you can access the beach. Just before you reach the wharf, turn **left**, staying on **355 East**. The road climbs slightly, and as you reach the top, sweeping views of Mira Bay reward you. The road traces the bay's outline, crossing towns and causeways. On weekends the road can be busy as local traffic shuttles between beaches and towns.

One of the most popular beaches is **Mira Beach**, at the mouth of the Mira River, 13.5 km from Main-à-Dieu. On a hot day, locals will bring their barbecues and lawn chairs and spend the day relaxing on the rocky banks of the Mira River.

From Mira Beach it is another 16 km to **Port Morien**, containing a jaunty port and a basic grocery store. Immediately after leaving Port Morien, keep right following Donkin Road. This next section of road follows Morien Bay. The Atlantic Ocean looms ahead, and on the surface of the dark water stands a lighthouse warning ships of Flint Island. The tour's most beautiful section follows windswept cliffs and open sea. Just 7 km from the junction with 255 you come to the town of **Donkin**; 4 km farther, you merge with **255 East**. The road skirts the Big Glace Bay Lake Bird Sanctuary, but the traffic begins to pick up as you near the city of Glace Bay. Regrettably, the scenery deteriorates quickly. About 6 km after merging with the highway, turn left on **Dominion Street**. This side road will skip the traffic mess of Glace Bay. In 4 km, this street merges with **Highway 4**. Stay on 4 and roll past the Sydney Airport and the University College of Cape Breton, and 9.5 km farther you pass 125 and enter the city. Only 4 km from the junction, you are back at the tour's starting point in downtown Sydney.

NEW BRUNSWICK

INTRODUCTION

Geography

New Brunswick's position in Atlantic Canada is unique. Since it's the only Maritime province bordering the United States, it has more in common with Maine than with Newfoundland. Maine sits to the west, the province of Quebec lies to the north, the Gulf of St. Lawrence and the Northumberland Strait lap at the eastern shore, and the Bay of Fundy's tides rise and fall on the west coast. The only connection it has to the rest of the Maritimes is the 30-km stretch of the Trantamar Marsh bordering Nova Scotia and the ferries from St. John to Digby, Nova Scotia, and from Tormentine to Borden, Prince Edward Island. Forest enshrouds 85 percent of the 73,000 square kilometers, and most

The hulls of discarded fishing boats lie forgotten near Castalia Harbour.

of the uninhabited interior is a barely accessible jumble of rocks, lakes, and trees. The encircling areas provide the best opportunities for cycling. The saw-toothed Bay of Fundy coast begins with steep northeastern terrain that discourages road construction, but south of St. John the gentle coast rolls over a mixed landscape. Chunks of islands, such as Grand Manan, Deer, and Campobello, lie in the southern reaches of Passamaquoddy Bay, and small fishing villages season the coast. The St. John River, the province's most important waterway, begins its serene journey in Maine, continues through fertile fields of potatoes, breaks only at turbulent Grand Falls, and finally empties into the Bay of Fundy at St. John. The Miramichi, the province's second-largest river, flows into the Gulf of St. Lawrence. Its route through forest-covered uplands attracts a brand of "testosterone" tourism based on hunting and fishing. The east coast, a low-lying marshland interspersed with Acadian forest of birch and pine, provided a home to the Acadian refugees after their expulsion in 1755 and provides a habitat for Kouchibouguac National Park, the most intriguing park in the province.

New Brunswick is a quiet, sparsely populated province. That's its charm. Fredericton, its capital, is home to only 46,000 people. Apart from the Trans-Canada Highway and Highway 11, the roads are sparsely traveled; traffic is rarely a problem. Most trips through the province are quiet and relaxing. The challenges come from the long isolated sections of rock and forest. Most of New Brunswick's terrain is flat to rolling with few steep or long hills. From the Bay of Chaleur to the Bay of Fundy and from the Northumberland Strait to Maine, New Brunswick offers quiet, comfortable riding.

History

New Brunswick has always been a mere land bridge in the political struggles for North America. The region's trails and portages, fashioned by the Maliseet and the Micmac through nearly impenetrable forests and lakes, were used by the troops of France and England to transport reinforcements and supplies to the battlegrounds of Quebec, Nova Scotia, and New England.

For thousands of years the Micmac and the Maliseet roamed over the area that would become New Brunswick. The Micmac, a nomadic tribe, followed game as they migrated. They set up winter camps based on family relationships and congregated in larger tribes. Come spring, hunting and fishing parties set out to hunt and gather for winter survival. The only difference between the Maliseet and Micmac was that the Maliseet practiced agriculture, planting crops for the coming winter. Later Europeans would call the natives "red skins" because of the natives' custom of rubbing red ochre on their bodies as an insect repellent, and rubbing it on their corpses for sacred reasons. Samuel de Champlain and Pierre Du Gua de Monts were the first documented Europeans to arrive in New Brunswick, and they set up their first camp on Ile de Croix, near today's St. Andrews. Unprepared for the harsh winter, many in the expedition died, and the explorers fled to Port Royal in Nova Scotia and settled there.

The French began to learn the locations of the portages and established small trading posts at native villages such as Meductic and St. Anne's. A few hundred French fur traders glibly felt they were masters of 32,000 square kilometers of territory. As word of this Arcadia spread, the French authorities began granting *signories*, large parcels of land that were given to the wealthy if they would develop it and bring settlers into the region. The first settlers who came started to settle on the lower St. John River and the east coast. The group began developing the land and their culture, eventually becoming the fateful Acadians. After the Acadians' deportation, many of the refugees fled north, up to the St. Léonard region on the St. John River and northeast near Shippagan and Caraquet. Forced to settle in the frequently flooded marshlands and more inaccessible areas of the province, they hoped they would be forgotten. However, led by General Wolfe, Colonel Monckton, vengeful British soldiers, and New England raiders who were gleeful at eliminating competition, the ragtag army continued to harry, round up, and expel the woeful Acadians. With the Treaty of Paris in 1763, after Quebec fell to Wolfe, Britain allowed the Acadians to return to their homeland with the condition that they disperse in small groups throughout the province. Today, French speakers compose one-third of the province's people and New Brunswick is Canada's only official bilingual province. For a poignant account of the Acadian exodus you can read Antonine Maillet's proud book, *Pélagie-la-Charrette*.

Settlers from England and Ireland began arriving in New Brunswick, but despite their hard work and the richness of the land they remained poor. Food from the crops, forest, and rivers was plentiful, but manufactured goods, such as carts and grindstones, had to be transported over formidable distances and costs were unmanageable. Speculators complicated settlement in New Brunswick. They grabbed the arable land and let it to immigrants, who would improve it. Then the speculators tried to sell it to new immigrants at inflated prices. The problem was the new immigrants didn't arrive, that is until the American War of Independence. New England residents who were dedicated to the monarchy were forced to leave their land and possessions in New York and New Jersey. The British government promised each refugee and soldier land of their own and tools. The population jumped tenfold as 14,000 refugees crossed the border.

The new population of Loyalists provided the impetus for New Brunswick to separate from the authority of distant Halifax. Feeling that the new land should be their private Elysium, they began the process of separation and prosperity.

The early 1800s was New Brunswick's most affluent era. The monopoly the region had over trading in the West Indies and Britain's duty on Baltic lumber, combined with the Napoleonic Wars, made New Brunswick affluent and industrious, so industrious that there were warnings of the forest's destruction and a need for conservation as early as 1810. Maine and New Brunswick had always fought over their exact boundaries. Quarrels and skirmishes broke out between lumber camps, and Maine contended most of the province's lumber and fertile river valley should belong to it. By the mid-1800s the boom times were over, but a new federalism marked by the pledge of an intercontinental railway, lower taxes, and a market for their raw materials enticed the residents of New Brunswick to vote for entry into the Confederation of Canada.

As the century rolled on, two populations divided the province, the impoverished French-speaking population of the north and east, and the prosperous English-speaking people of the west and south. At the turn of the century, New Brunswickers trundled along, dealing with the two issues of bilingualism and an economy that began to show its lack of diversity. Today, entrepreneurial spirit and extensive government grants have made the province one of the communications-development capitals in Canada. Its diversity is seen in its food processing plants, telecommunications center, and transport industry. The near extinction of groundfish and the collapse of the fisheries haven't affected the province as they have in Newfoundland and Nova Scotia. Of all the

Old fish stores and the Wood Island Lighthouse at Wood Island ferry terminal

Atlantic provinces, New Brunswick is the healthiest economically. However, it is still Canada's have-not province and still requires a heavy dose of federal transfer payments to stay healthy.

Weather

New Brunswick is Atlantic Canada's warmest province. Because the sea has less influence on most of the land mass, the interior can be sultry. The warm air of late spring and early summer, combined with the frigid waters of the Bay of Fundy, can produce fog banks that last up to a week while a few kilometers inland the weather is warm and sunny. Bringing a flashing rear light to use if you ride in such weather is a good idea. Prevailing winds shift from the southwest to northwest as you travel farther north. On the south coast most of the weather influences come from the American Midwest, while the northern portion of the province is influenced by central Canada and Arctic air masses. Most of the province's rain falls during the spring. Poor weather usually accompanies easterly winds.

Autumn is a perfect time for cycling in New Brunswick. The red, yellow, and orange colors of the changing leaves on the Kingston Peninsula and the St. John River Valley create an explosion of colors in the lucent air. Bugs, which are a nuisance in the summer, dissipate during the cooler months of September. The only disadvantage to autumn is that many services and attractions close after the first weekend of September.

Accommodations

Along most of the province's main routes, you can find hotels and motels, but far more interesting are the family-run establishments such as cottages and bed and breakfasts. During the high season, it's a good idea to reserve ahead, which you can do at any provincial tourist office or by using the Dial-a-Nite service that connects with the province's licensed establishments. Yet it's usual to pass by small homes in remote areas that offer cheap and friendly accommodations to travelers.

Provincial and national parks do not allow reservations for camping. Every lot is on a first-come/first-served basis, and during the high season demand can be high. For example, at Kouchibouguac National Park, the waiting list starts by 9:00 A.M. Luckily, cyclists can use the primitive sites at a fraction of the price. Provincial park campgrounds seem to be located at tourist resorts such as beaches and other recreational areas. Normally, you can't rely solely on provincial parks to pitch your tent. Usually they're inconveniently spread throughout the province.

Private campground prices are based on the services they provide. Some take reservations, others won't. Scattered randomly, they could be on an unused portion of a farmer's field or at a seaside resort. For a comprehensive list of accommodations pick up a listing at any New Brunswick tourist office.

TOUR NO. 9

THE FUN FUNDY BAY

Start / Finish: St. John/St. Stephen
Distance: 213.4 kilometers (130 miles)
Estimated time: 3 days
Terrain: Level to slightly hilly
Map: New Brunswick Travel Map
Connecting tours: Tour No. 10
Connections: Highways 102, 3, 9; Interstate I-95
from Calais, Maine

Highway 1 is a small but busy portion of this tour. Cross-border shoppers regularly scoot along it in their mad dash for bargains. Vacationers beeline along it to pass quickly through St. John, Fundy National Park, and eventually Prince Edward Island, and trucks rumble goods between the United States and Canada. But off Highway 1, you'll find a series of headlands and islands removed from the bustle of the main highway. At Maces Bay you'll find views that stretch out to open sea. At Blacks Harbour you'll hear the cacophony of gulls fighting over the entrails of gutted fish. Blacks Harbour is also the terminus for the ferry to Grand Manan, an isolated island that's a throwback to quieter, simpler times. Past Blacks Harbour you'll enter Loyalist country, where British flags still fly and the villages, resorts, and border towns string along the coast.

The longest stretch without supplies is the 40 km from St. John to Lepreau, otherwise supplies are regular. The only reliable bike shop is in St. John. The climate is temperate, but it can be foggy for days at a time.

This is the easiest tour in New Brunswick. Spruce and fir forests, broken by farmland, roll along the roads. Hills are slight. The views are enthralling, and finding provisions is rarely a problem. There is lots to see and do along the Bay of Fundy; the only nuisance is Highway 1.

St. John to New River Beach Provincial Park: 64.8 kilometers

Before you leave St. John try to take a couple of the downtown St. John walking tours, described in brochures available at the Tourist Office. The bike tour begins at the Tourist Office and follows Main Street under the pedestrian overpass. After 1.4 km, turn **left** at **Chesley Drive**, following the signs for 100 West. You pass Reversing Falls, and after 3.5 km, turn **right** following **100 West**. After 2.2 km, turn **left**,

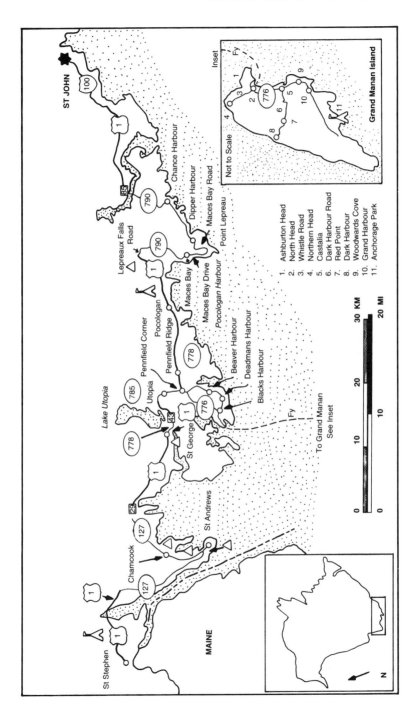

Inset

Grand Manan Island

Not to Scale

Fy

776

1. Ashburton Head
2. North Head
3. Whistle Road
4. Northern Head
5. Castalia
6. Dark Harbour Road
7. Red Point
8. Dark Harbour
9. Woodwards Cove
10. Grand Harbour
11. Anchorage Park

ST JOHN

Chance Harbour

Dipper Harbour

Maces Bay Road

Point Lepreau

Lepreaux Falls Road

Maces Bay

Maces Bay Drive

Pocologan Harbour

Pennfield Corner

Pocologan

Pennfield Ridge

Beaver Harbour

Deadmans Harbour

Blacks Harbour

Lake Utopia

Utopia

St George

To Grand Manan

See Inset

Fy

St Andrews

Chamcook

St Stephen

MAINE

N

30 KM

20 MI

0   10   20

0   10   20

staying on the main road that follows the escarpment overlooking the bay. After 500 meters, you come to Exit 97, which you do not take, but rather **merge** with **Highway 1** after another 2.3 km. Through this next section of Highway 1, a four-lane divided highway remains fairly level as it passes the shores of Spruce and Ludgate lakes. Otherwise, Highway 1 follows a nondescript deforested area. Thankfully, you leave this sterile road after 15.3 km, where you exit **right** at **Exit 85** for **790**. The official name for this area is Musquash, but expect no settlement. At the top of the overpass, 300 meters farther, turn **left** onto **790** toward Chance Harbour. As soon as you leave Highway 1, the cycling conditions improve. The trees become intimate friends, brooks rush under the road to greet you, and even a waterfall thunders your arrival. Take a deep breath—relax. After 10 km of ideal cycling, you come to the small village of **Chance Harbour**, which has a small general store. As you leave this hamlet, the road follows the enthralling coastline of Little Dipper Harbour. The sea along this section acts like a lover—during low periods, it's untouchable, but when it's high, the water lovingly caresses the shore. After 9 km of this coastline, you come to another idyllic fishing village, **Dipper Harbour**, named after a species of duck that dips when it catches its prey. After 2.3 km, turn **left** onto **Maces Bay Road**. The road is unmarked; identify it by the school on your right and the baseball field on your left. This short road is one of the most satisfying of the tour. Continue past the STOP sign, and after 1.8 km switch back. The seascape explodes in front of you. Sharp cliffs jut out to sea, and exposed boulders play hide-and-seek with the tides. Across the bay you can see proud islands and the stoic mainland.

This area, **Point Lepreau**, used to be a native hunting area. For thousands of years, aboriginal people would camp and hunt porpoises during summers, but today it's the site of Atlantic Canada's first nuclear power plant. After 2.5 km, turn **left** at the T and follow **Maces Bay Drive**. The road changes character quickly. Although still an oceanside drive, you now pass the summer homes of St. John residents. After about 4.5 km, you turn **left** onto gently rolling **790 West**. In less than 2 km **Hanson Stream Picnic Area**, a handsome little park, springs upon you. After another 1.7 km turn **left** onto **Lepreaux Falls Road**, and about 1 km farther you arrive at **Lepreaux Falls**. Considering the lack of publicity, the falls are surprisingly dramatic. Cascading in two sections, the river drops and winds into a picturesque valley covered in spruce and then continues its restless journey. Beyond the falls 500 meters turn **left**, returning to **Highway 1**, which has made a disconcerting change from a four-lane divided highway to a two-lane, almost shoulder-less, ribbon of speed. For 6 km, follow Highway 1 to **New River Beach Provincial Park**, which has camping and an expansive crescent of sand.

New River Beach Provincial Park to Anchorage Provincial Park: 48.8 kilometers plus side trips

The earlier you're on Highway 1 the less traffic you'll find on the road. From the park it's a 10.5-km ride to the village of Pocologan (full provisions). The road, probably the prettiest part of Highway 1, skirts **Maces Bay** and **Pocologan Harbour**. During low tides, you'll see clam diggers burrowing in the tide-packed sand. The route continues to be flat as you pass the village of **Pennfield Ridge**. The terrain surrounding this area once had an airfield, but it has been taken over by organized drag, stock-car, and mud-pit racing. Every Sunday at the local fire hall, volunteer firefighters serve breakfast for the racers, spectators, and wayward bike tourists. Past Pocologan 14.5 km, you arrive at Pennfield Corner and the junction to **776 South**. Turn **left**, and after another 100 meters turn **right**, staying on **776**. This quiet road rolls through wood lots and farm country as it skips along for 9 km to **Blacks Harbour**. Your nose might sense the town before your eyes as Blacks Harbour is the center of Canada's sardine industry.

At the tourist office (open between June 15 and September 3) try to pick up a copy of *Heritage Trails and Footpaths*, describing Grand Manan's nineteen hiking trails. If you don't obtain a copy here, the next copies will be at Grand Harbour, halfway down the island.

The terminal for the Grand Manan ferry is 2 km from Blacks Harbour's center. If you are in a car, arrive at least 45 minutes early from the scheduled departure times as there will be a line for boarding. If

Fishing boats moored at North Harbour on Grand Manan

you're arriving by bike, don't worry. Rarely will you be unable to get on. Apparently, Transport Canada does random checks of the number of passengers, but the crews normally limit just the number of vehicles. During the summer six ferries run daily for the 2-hour ride.

Grand Manan, the Bay of Fundy's largest island, has attracted naturalists for its bird and sea life, geologists for its 900-million-year-old rock strata, artists for its inspiring seascapes and solitude, and vacationers for its unhurried pace of life. As the ferry makes its journey across the waters, porpoises play in the boat's wake, and farther off whales cautiously measure the boat's presence. The tourists become excited as the boat nears the island and the craggy cliffs of Ashburton Head and North Head rise into view. Finally, the boat veers around the sentinel, Swallowtail Lighthouse, and cozies up to the small harbor of North Head. Be careful when leaving the ferry; the crew may ask you to wait until all the vehicles have left. Trundle up to the end of the ferry road and turn **left** onto **776**, the island's principal road. Quickly, you are in the calm village of **North Head**. After about 2 km, you come to **Whistle Road** that heads to **Ashburton Head**. Along this road, near the Marathon Hotel, you can see the curious geological formations of Old Bishop and Hole-in-the-Wall, masses of traprock shaped by the wind and sea. Farther along this road lies a 900-million-year-old rock strata named after the creation story in the Bible, The 7 Days' Work.

Back on **776**, 6 km along this gentle shore road you come to the village of **Castalia** (full provisions). To the right is the road to the ominous village of Dark Harbour. If you follow this side road, the character of the island changes. From a gently sloping land supporting farms and cottages, the landscape becomes more austere—craggy and desolate—the result of a volcanic eruption 16 million years ago. From **Red Point** the road drops into **Dark Harbour**, a village surrounded by 91-meter-high cliffs. Although the sun may not shine on the cliffs until noon, residents swear that's not why the town got its name.

Back on 776 it's only a short 500 meters until you reach the junction for the gravel road leading to Castalia Marsh. This picnic and bird-viewing site is an ideal area to watch for the 245 species of birds that migrate to and live in the area. In 1833, the artist John James Audubon was in awe of this area as he observed the multitude of birds and worked on the island.

After less than 3 km you pass **Woodwards Cove**. Across the harbor, notice the shacks used for smoking herring. During the season, smoke billowing from the smoldering sawdust cures the herring draped over the sheds' racks. Another 3 km and you come to **Grand Harbour** and **Grand Manan Museum**.

The museum features natural history, geological, and historical exhibits, and a separate wing for the Allen L. Moses stuffed bird collection. The collection of over 3,000 birds was assembled by Moses, an internationally renowned naturalist who, despite stuffing so many birds, saved the eider duck from extinction.

About 4 km from Grand Harbour, you arrive at the junction for **Anchorage Provincial Park**, 1.3 km to the **left**. Seal Cove Beach, less than a km farther down the road, has a bed and breakfast.

Anchorage Provincial Park to St. Stephen: 99.8 kilometers

Return the approximately 16 km along **776** to **North Head Ferry**. After disembarking from the ferry on the mainland, continue 2 km back along 776. Turn **right** along **778 West**. The next section of the road is the tour's steepest section. If you want to avoid it, stay on 776 back to Highway 1. As you pass appropriately named **Deadmans Harbour**, 778 begins scaling the first of the short, sheer hills. After 6.2 km you come to **Beaver Harbour**.

Throughout this area, aquaculture is becoming big business. Salmon, surviving easily in captivity, were one of the first cultured fish, and now salmon farming sites nestle in almost every bay, cove, and inlet, including Beaver Harbour. Aquaculture is starting to pay large dividends to those taking their chances against disease, poaching, and "superfreeze," when the sea water begins to congeal, freezing hundreds of thousands of fingerlings.

Another 6 km from Beaver Harbour, and you arrive back at **Pennfield Corner**. Over Highway 1, continue **straight** on **Highway 785**. After about 5 km, passing by the settlement of **Utopia**, keep **left** on **785**. The road now follows the shores of Lake Utopia.

After 3 km, you join with **Highway 1** again and turn **right**. But in only 700 meters turn **left** at **Exit 43** on **778 South**. Suddenly, you are on a quiet, residential street in **St. George**, and after 1.2 km, you arrive at St. George's granite post office.

St. George was once known as Granite Town. In the 1800s, quarries flourished, supplying stone for Boston Cathedral, New York's Museum of Natural History, and Ottawa's Parliament buildings. The industry died in the 1920s when stone was no longer architecturally fashionable.

The most picturesque sight in town is the red mill, self-assuredly balanced on the lip of the gorge. Today, the mill is a generating plant owned by the Irving conglomerate. The Magaguadavic (pronounced mag-ga-dave-y) Falls provide a perfect spot to generate electricity, but are a major obstacle for Atlantic salmon struggling to swim upriver to spawn.

From the intersection with the post office continue **right** along **Main Street** and after 200 meters, before you cross the bridge over the falls, you come to the St. George Fishway Salmon Ladders. During the spawning season, you can watch the silver fish leap from one pool to the next, finally making their way to the calmer section upriver. Walk down the iron stairway to the viewing windows to witness the salmon's instinctual struggle against the river forces. Even if the salmon are not spawning, take a look in the windows, as other fish could be in the swirling currents.

Continuing along Main Street for about 2 km, you come back to **Highway 1**. Turn **left**. The level road continues for 11 km until you take **Exit 29 left** on **127**. Immediately, hills greet you. If you did not take 778 from Blacks Harbour, the next section will be the most hilly of the tour. The road through this section rolls through spruce and fir forest, and at a couple of points, the bay's water laps near the road. After 11 km, you arrive at **Chamcook** and the Atlantic Salmon Centre. As the brochure states, this new center "celebrates the life of the salmon and its role in the economy and history of the Maritimes." The best part of the center is the viewing chamber and the in-stream observation window. From Chamcook stay **left** at **Eddy's Corner** following 127 for another 2.3 km.

An inscription on a tombstone in the St. Andrews cemetery

As you slip down 127, you'll pass **Tara Manor**, guest home of the rich and famous, and after another 100 meters the gravel road to your left leads to Minister's Island. During high tide, this strait is under 3 meters of water, but during low tide it's possible to visit this charming little island. On it, Van Horne, the primary engineer for the transcontinental Canadian Pacific Railway, built his baronial mansion. At certain times, tourists are allowed to visit the manor; if you can't, it's still a unique experience to ride your bike over the sea bed.

From Eddy's Corner it's about 3 km to the junction with 127 (where you will eventually leave town), and it's only another 200 meters straight to **St. Andrews' tourist office**. St. Andrews, recently adding the romantic moniker "by-the-sea," was Canada's first seaside resort.

Of the 250 homes in town, 100 are over a century old. At the tourist office, pick up a copy of *A Guide to Historic St. Andrews*, which describes a walking tour through town, highlighting the historic buildings. Some of these are the Loyalist cemetery with its mournful inscriptions; Greenoak Presbyterian Church, built from the quick temper of an enraged sea captain; the court house, a surprisingly large neo-classical building; Canada's first prefab homes, brought section by section on barge from Maine; and Water Street, the town's bustling main thoroughfare. This area attracts bus tourists, campers, sailors, and Boston and New York sophisticates. St. Andrews-by-the-Sea offers numerous things to see and do, so plan on spending a few hours.

The road out of St. Andrews is less hilly. Turn **left** following **127**. As you cycle along a ridge you'll see Greenslaw Mountain, Simpson Hill, and Wiley's Mountain to your right and to your left, on the American side, Doucet's Island. Also named St. Croix Island, the Champlain and de Monts expedition spent its first disastrous winter in 1604 on this small piece of land.

You arrive back at Highway 1 after 16 km and then turn **left**. The route becomes messier beyond this point. Crosswinds blow across the bays, truck trailers' backdrafts suck you into the road, and gravel scatters over the road's shoulder. After about 5 km, you reach **Oak Bay Provincial Park** and campground. From Oak Bay, you enter the sprawling commercial suburbia of **St. Stephen** and pass a long strip of fast-food stands and car dealerships. After about 7.5 km, you turn **left** on **King Street**. Following straight-as-a-mast King Street, after 1.2 km you turn **right** onto **Milltown Boulevard**, and in 700 meters you arrive at the bridge over to Calais, Maine.

St. Stephen was not named in honor of a saint but facetiously for a rowdy member of an early surveying team. At one time, town officials tried to change the name to Dover, attempting to re-create the towns of France and England.

The amiability between St. Stephen and Calais has never been threatened, even during periods of war. In 1812 Canada and the United States were in armed conflict. The British authorities sent a cache of gunpowder to the border town to help its defense. The St. Stephen's residents, wondering what to do with the explosives, lent the cache to Calais for its 4th of July celebrations. The citizens of both towns refused to fight each other and trade across the border continued. Even today, the towns share each other's water supply, celebrate each other's holidays, and answer each other's fire alarms.

As you ride along Milltown Boulevard you pass the Chocolatier, the boutique selling world-famous Ganong chocolates. The Ganong family were chocolate moguls who were so exacting in their hand dipping that they imported specially trained women from Europe to produce the candies. Ganong bought Park Hall in 1900 to board the female workers known as Ganong Girls. Today, we have the Ganong family to thank for the chocolate bar, which Mr. Ganong invented as a snack for his fishing trips, the all-day sucker, and the heart-shaped valentine box. If you stop by the boutique you can stuff yourself with exquisite chocolates to celebrate the tour's end.

TOUR NO. 10

KINGSTON

Start / Finish: St. John/St. John
Distance: 285.3 kilometers (174 miles)
Estimated time: 4 days
Terrain: Hilly
Map: New Brunswick Travel Map
Connecting tours: Tour Nos. 9 and 11
Connections: Highway 2 and Highway 1 via St. John

The Kingston area of New Brunswick lies forgotten. Trees and brush shroud the small, weathered buildings turning gray with age. Languidly, cattle and horses graze in pastures still owned by Loyalist descendants. A century ago, the area was bustling. The residents dammed every brook for grist mills to grind grain and sawmills to cut lumber—goods the workers and farmers shipped down the river to St. John and Europe. Steamboats, a popular form of entertainment, would cruise the tranquil waterways and stop for the night at the romantic inns on the river banks. Today, as you cycle through this unforgettably quiet area, small reminders hint at this animated past: a covered bridge, the oldest church in New Brunswick, active artisans reviving a town, and stories of brash privateers.

The land is hilly. Past farmers cleared any level land for pasture and cultivation. On the hillsides, tinkling streams weave down the thicketed hillsides. If you love solitude, this tour, within minutes of St. John, will provide the quietest cycling in New Brunswick. Stock up on provisions when you can, as there are stretches on the Kingston and Wickham peninsulas where finding supplies is difficult. The only bike shop is in St. John. The climate is generally warm, with prevailing winds from the southwest.

St. John to Hampton: 73.2 kilometers

The tour begins at the tourist office in downtown St. John at the corner of **Water and St. Patrick streets**. Head **northeast** under the pedestrian overpass, keeping Market Square to your left. Carefully, continue over the viaduct and the Trans-Canada Highway, following the signs for 100 West to Reversing Falls. St. Patrick becomes **Main Street**. After 1.4 km, turn **right** on **Landsdowne**, and after another 600 meters, turn **left** on **Visart Road**. Stay on Visart for only 100 meters then turn **right** at **Churchill Boulevard**. After passing a residential development, you begin climbing the tour's first hill. Although the

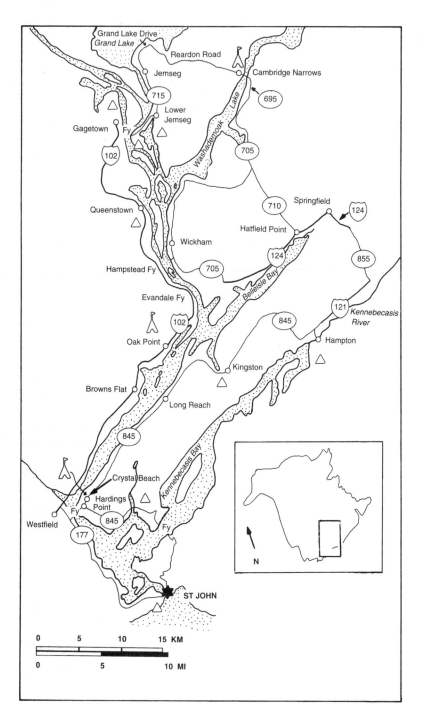

climb lasts only a kilometer, the landscape transforms. The land turns from flat harbor to rock and forest; the development disappears, and the next major settlement lays 70 km away. After about 3 km, Churchill Boulevard merges into **Sandy Point Road**. As the road winds through the forest and past cottages, you pass the hospital and Rockwood Golf Course. After about 2.5 km, turn **left**, staying on **Sandy Point Road**. Less than 100 meters beyond, to your right, is the Cherry Brook Zoo, which has a meager collection of local and exotic animals. After 500 meters, turn **left** at **Kennebecasis Drive**, and in another 600 meters turn **right** for the **ferry dock** which is another 100 meters farther.

The *Romeo and Juliet* is one of the free ferries used as part of New Brunswick's highway system. This ferry operates Monday to Saturday 6:00 A.M. to midnight, and Sundays and holidays 7:00 A.M. to midnight, leaving on the half hour.

From the ferry dock on the Kingston peninsula side you have a steep ride up to a T **intersection** about a km up the road. Keep **right**. After 1.3 km, turn **left** onto **845 West**. As you climb and roll past the lacy streams flowing through the forest, the sharp smell of pine seasoned with the cozy smell of wood fires from the small cottages fills the air. After about 4 km, you come to the only covered bridge on this tour, the Milkish Inlet #1.

The word *milkish* is derived from the Maliseet *a-mil-kesh*, meaning "a drying place." For 3,500 years the Paleo-Indians and Maliseets used the area to dry the fish and meat they hunted in the prolific St. John waters and forest. It wasn't until 1758 that the area saw its first non-indigenous settlers, a group of Black Loyalists.

After crossing the bridge, turn **left**, continuing on **845 West**. As you cross, admire the views of the Champlain Mountains. After 9.5 km, you reach the junction for the Westfield ferry and Kingston. Down to your left 1 km is **Hardings Point** (provisions). Turn **right**, staying on **845**. Another 200 meters up the road is the turn for **Crystal Beach**. The road along this section is less hilly as it follows a ridge above the Long Reach body of water, and after 17 km, you arrive at the village of **Long Reach** (general store). From the road you can see Caton's Island, Isle of Pines, and Rocky Island sitting in the river. After Long Reach, the road levels, except for a climb over Shampers Bluff, after which it follows a stretch of road beside Kingston Creek. Steeply, the road rises up Kingston Hill to arrive, after a total of 14 km, at the interesting town of **Kingston** (grocery).

Kingston remains a bulwark for Loyalist tradition. After the British enacted the Stamp Act in 1765, frustrated New England colonists focused their hostility on anything British. Seizing the moment, the Whig part of Connecticut—which had always abhorred the Anglican Church for praying for the king and the royal family—stoked the New England colonists' frustration. This frustration hardened into hatred and intense persecution of Anglicans. Anglican churches were stoned and forced to close. The clergy became villains and the Whig party the vigilantes. The Loyalists were forced to abandon everything. Most of the Loyalists who settled in the Kingston area were farmers from southwestern Connecticut, and it was their community solidarity, welded by their experiences of persecution, that helped them to proudly erect the Trinity Anglican Church and Rectory in 1789. Today it's the oldest church in New Brunswick that is still on its original foundations.

Across the street from the church, the John Fisher Memorial Museum is located in the school.

From the intersection where the church, school, and gas station face each other, continue **straight** on **845**, keeping the gas station to your left. As you leave town you pass the Kingston farmer's market, held every Saturday morning in the summer. This quiet road rolls along gentle hills, squeezing around the highest ones. When you squirt out the other side of the peninsula you cycle along a small bluff of the Pickwauket Mountain overlooking Kennebecasis Bay. After 18 km, you come to the junction of Highway 121. About 800 meters to your **right** is **Hampton**. As you cycle into town you pass a restaurant, grocery, and faded homes. King's County Museum, containing photos, documents, early furniture, and jail cells, is about 2.5 km from the intersection.

Hampton to Cambridge Narrows: 88.3 kilometers

From the center of Hampton **return** to the junction with **845** and continue **straight** along **121 East**. This section of road has to follow a bluff because of the yearly freshet that overflows the Kennebecasis River. Across the river you can hear the roar of traffic along the Trans-Canada Highway, and if you're up early you may see a deer on the roadside or in the marshes. The road remains fairly level, passing by dairy farms, small houses, and quaint barns. Past the junction 8 km, turn **left** on **855** toward Springfield. From the junction you face a long, 2.5-km climb over the peninsula, and then the road rolls to **124** where 855 merges 9 km from the junction with 121. Stay on 124 to **Springfield** about 1.5 km farther. In Springfield (full provisions) keep **left** on **124**. About 6 km farther you arrive at **Hatfield Point** (store). The road follows Belleisle Bay until it veers inland, climbs over a hill, and then drops back to the shore. Stay on 124 East. After passing a junction to another ferry, and after 7 km, the road crosses a series of tightly bunched, steep hills, but the views over Belleisle Bay make the effort worthwhile. The bay was named for Alexandre Le Borgne de Belleisle, an Acadian who lived on its shore in the early 1700s. After another 7.5 km, turn **right** on **705 West** for Wickham. The solitude through this area is striking. Few cars roar by to disturb you, few people work the fields; you're alone, but if you need company, you can look over the ponds for beaver lodges.

Highway 705 through this area rolls over some spicy hills. As you near Wickham you pass the aptly named Spoon Island. After 9.5 km, you pass the ferry for Hampstead, and after 2.3 km, you pass the settlement of **Wickham** (no provisions).

After Wickham the road rolls along pastureland where cows and horses graze contentedly. For the first 7 km the road rocks gently and then it starts rolling more severely. About 21 km from Wickham, turn **left** on **710**. This road follows a river valley lush with thick forest and dotted with farms, providing views of Washademoak Lake. After another 14.5 km turn **left** on **695**. Cross over the bridge, and 1.5 km farther you're at **Cambridge Narrows**.

Cambridge Narrows is a cottage community servicing the area's 400 to 500 summer cottages. As the owner of the grocery told me, "If there are any tourists around here, they're lost. There's nothing 'round here but quiet." I thought, "Perfect."

Cambridge Narrows to Oak Point Provincial Park: 75.1 kilometers

From Cambridge Narrows stay on 695 which scales Den Brook Valley, and after 9 km turn **right** on **Reardon Road** toward Grand Lake. After 1.4 km, you come to the shoreline and turn **left** onto **Grand Lake Drive**.

After about 7.5 km and one hill, turn **left** over Highway 2. After another km you arrive at the junction of 695 and 715 and the community of **Jemseg** (grocery). Turn **right** onto **715**. As you cross the next section, listen for the booming sounds of the artillery practicing at the firing ranges of Canadian Forces Base Gagetown. The road follows a gently sloping valley covered in spruce trees and punctuated by apple orchards and strawberry fields.

In Jemseg and Lower Jemseg look for houses with "mother-in-law steps." By not putting in steps and leaving their homes technically unfinished, the locals avoided the higher taxes on finished homes.

Past Jemseg 7 km you arrive in **Lower Jemseg**, a small settlement bordering the road. On your left look for an old Baptist church, beaten gray by the elements. It's now used for storing potatoes. Once scheduled for demolition, it was bought and saved by the family across the road. Another 200 meters down the road is the interesting Trinity Anglican Church. This small church is unusual for the area since it's made of stone. The window and door casings were brought over from Normandy, France, and were left over from Christ Church Cathedral in Fredericton. Usually, the church is open for visitors to admire the cozy interior.

Past the church 100 meters turn **right** onto **Ferry Road**. You pass a cairn with a cannonball on top of it. In 1659 Lower Jemseg was a British trading post but was ceded to France in 1667 and then pillaged and dismantled in 1674 by Dutch and American privateers. The cannonball is rumored to be from the battle even though the governor surrendered without firing a shot.

The road to the ferry is an ideal spot for birdwatching. Birds float their songs across the ponds and thickets. Bright yellow warblers flash, and luminous red vireos agilely flit between branches. High atop electric poles, osprey nest and perch, surveying the area. Everywhere you look you spot more birds. The skittish blue heron takes off in long graceful strokes while stubby-winged teals frantically splash across the glassy water. The 4-km ride to the ferry ends too quickly.

The ferry runs as it's needed, so ring for service if it's on the other side.

Past the ferry dock 700 meters, turn right on **102** for **Gagetown** a km farther.

Poor, misunderstood Gagetown. One hot summer day, an Army battalion came rumbling into town. Replete with transports, jeeps, and tanks mounted on trailers, they halted on the main street. Bewildered, one of the soldiers asked an equally confused resident for directions to the HQ. The village of Gagetown was confused with the military base of CFB Gagetown centered in Oromocto.

In the middle of another hot, dry spell the Army was practicing heavy artillery firing and managed to ignite an immense area of grassland. Thick black smoke suffocated the town for days. Recently, politicians thought Gagetown was a perfect site for a PCB incinerator, but residents put up a heated protest. The residents have become a driving force in the community, which has become a retreat for artists, artisans, and actors. The modest galleries and studios contain some of the best artwork in New Brunswick, and the town is gaining prominence. The town follows a dramatic cycle of ups and downs. Now it's on the upswing. Plan to spend a few hours browsing though the shops and visiting the Queens County Museum, the birthplace of a Father of Confederation, Sir Samuel Tilley. Even the Victorian Post Office is worth a look to admire the brass fittings and mailboxes. Moreover, visit the Loomcrofters, a small loom studio housed in the oldest building still in use in New Brunswick.

Gagetown was a major stopover during the age of steam, and the Steamer Stop Inn, still in operation, is worth looking in for its decor and river view. The owner may rent you a canoe so you can explore a part of the river, particularly Mount House on Grimross Island.

From the junction with **102**, **return south**. For the next 9.5 km, you have a gentle ascent to the top of Onataga Hill. Be careful on the searing, 1 km, 8-percent downhill. After the drop, you enter a wide valley, eventually following the main flow of the St. John River. The road continues to be hilly, but it does offer sublime views over the river. After another 5.5 km, you pass **Queenstown** and McKinney's General Store. Stop and look at this dying breed of store. Although the McKinneys no longer own this melange of goods, the store is full of nostalgia. Originally bought by James McKinney in 1922, the building was dragged across the frozen river by oxen from Wickham one cold winter day in 1910.

The road's next section rolls slightly as it flows beside the riverbank. It can be rough in spots due to flooding. From Queenstown 9 km, you pass the **Hampstead ferry** and after another 7 km the **Evandale ferry**. Neither spot has provisions. South of Evandale the road follows the Long Reach, flanked by impressive hills covered in hardwood and

Opposite: *The lighthouse at Oak Point Provincial Park*

laced with trout streams. The last section before Oak Point follows a section of river known as Mistake Cove. Edward Coy from Connecticut sailed up this dead-end channel in 1763, mistakenly thinking he was on the right course. The name stuck. From Evandale it's 11 km to the junction of Oak Point Provincial Park, a km to your left. Oak Point has tree-shaded campsites, showers, a beach, and at the end of the park an obelisk-shaped lighthouse.

Oak Point Provincial Park to St. John: 48.7 kilometers

Back on 102, about 7.5 km from the junction to Oak Point along a hilly road, you come to **Browns Flat** (provisions). Along the way you'll see expansive views over the channels and islands of the St. John River.

From Browns Flat, traffic begins to increase. After a 2-km, 6-percent descent, the land becomes flat with a few hills. After 16 km, you turn **left** on **177**. Following the sign for Grand Bay, after 2.3 km you come to the road for the Hardings Point ferry. (Highway 177 has a paved shoulder into St. John, but if you want a more quiet ride back to St. John, you could return by way of 845 and Milkish Creek.) While on 177 watch for gravel and cracks in the road. After 7.3 km, turn **left** on **River Road**, passing by the St. John marina. After another 17 km, turn **left** onto **Dever Road**, which merges into **Church Street**. After 1.8 km, turn **left** onto **Bridge Road**, and after 200 meters turn **left** at the lights on **Main Street**. The names of the streets seem to change every block so just continue along the main road for 600 meters until you turn **left** on **Bridge Road**. After 0.5 km, you come to **Reversing Falls**.

The falls are a natural phenomenon, and it is said that Glooscap, the Micmac god, helped create the oddity. During low tides, the St. John River flows down though its normal course, but when the tide changes and the powerful Bay of Fundy tides pour in, the water direction changes, and the water begins flowing upriver over the same falls. The tides have impressed every group who has seen it for centuries.

From Reversing Falls turn **left** after 300 meters onto **Douglas Street**. After 1.3 km, you pass the **New Brunswick Provincial Museum**, containing natural history and displays about the lives of First Nations people, French, British, and other settlers of the province. After 800 meters, turn **right** onto **Main Street**, arriving back at the tourist office.

TOUR NO. 11

THE ST. JOHN RIVER

Start / Finish: Fredericton/Grand Falls
Distance: 280.9 kilometers (171 miles)
Estimated time: 3 days
Terrain: Slightly hilly
Map: New Brunswick Travel Map
Connecting tours: Tour Nos. 10 and 12
Connections: Trans-Canada Highway 2

For thousands of years the St. John River has been a principal Maritimes travel route. In the pre-European era, the Maliseet camped and lived on the river banks, while their adversaries, the Mohawks, used the river route to raid the Maliseet. In the seventeenth century the French *signeurs*, who by then owned most of the river, gathered furs from the Maliseet to pay for France's extravagance. In the eighteenth century the St. John became the main route between Quebec and the Fortress of Louisbourg and French authorities scoured its tributaries to recruit First Peoples to help raid New England towns. Later, under British rule, the river carried larger craft from the interior. It also acted as the mail route between Halifax and Quebec. In the nineteenth century logging grew into an economic mainstay. Wild and lawless lumberjacks clearcut centuries-old pines and then sent them downriver in tremendous log booms. Today, the Trans-Canada Highway, carrying the province's economy on its back, slides beside this serene river. But on the other bank, a system of forgotten roads roll beside the river—perfect for cycling. Supplies are easy to obtain throughout the tour, but the only bike shop is in Fredericton. The weather is usually warm with winds from the southwest shifting to the north as you travel upriver. Morning fog patches are possible, and bugs can be a nuisance.

This tour incorporates only 40 km of the Trans-Canada Highway, the busiest section of the tour, and that's so you can visit King's Landing, New Brunswick's most impressive tourist attraction. Otherwise, the roads offer a sense of solitude, sweeping through birch and balsam forests sprinkled with fiddlehead ferns and quilted with potato fields. From Fredericton to Grand Falls, you're never far from a town that brims with colorful stories, tall legends, and historical significance—all within the backdrop of the majestic St. John River Valley.

Fredericton to Nackawic: 75.3 kilometers

Fredericton, New Brunswick's capital city, sits on a wide section of the river. Originally called St. Anne by the Acadians, the incoming Loyalists changed it to Fredericton in honor of King George III's brother. Today, this low-lying town supports about 50,000 people, many of them service and government workers. A few of the city's highlights include the Beaverbrook Art Gallery, Guard House, Soldiers' Barracks, and Christ Church Cathedral. The tourist office offers extensive information about

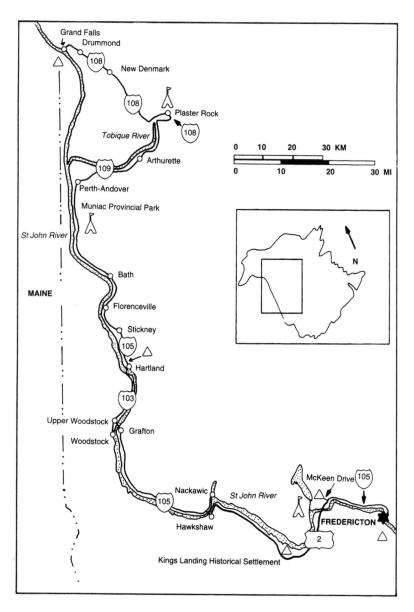

the city's sights, and if you want to explore more remote areas, pick up the pamphlet *Trail Guidelines*, which describes the city's hiking and biking trails.

The bike tour starts in front of City Hall at **York and Queen streets**. Head east for 150 meters where you turn **right** onto **West-moreland Avenue** and then cross the bridge over the St. John River. After 800 meters follow the signs for 105 South as you veer **right** toward **Main Street**, and after another 900 meters turn **left** onto **Main**. **Highway 105 South** begins as you turn **left** after another 2.7 km. During the morning rush, this road can be busy but most of the traffic is heading into town. You leave the city and the road undulates slightly as you pass small riverfront homes. After the intersection for 104, hills become more feisty. Staying on 105, about 20 km from the merge, you come to **McKeen Drive**. To your left 1.5 km is Tula Farms, an example of Nigerian farming techniques practiced in Atlantic Canada.

About 2.5 km along merge **right** onto **Trans-Canada Highway 2**. Although I don't like major highways, this road's shoulder is wide and safe. Furthermore, it's the only route to King's Landing. After another 9 km you pass Woolastook Wildlife Park and Campground. From the junction with the park you immediately cross Longs Creek Bridge. Be careful on this narrow bridge as it lacks a shoulder or walkway. After 6.5 km turn **right** at **Exit 259** to **King's Landing Historical Settlement**, and 200 meters farther, turn **right** into the parking lot.

King's Landing flourishes as a convincing re-creation of a nineteenth-century New Brunswick farming settlement. Seventy fully furnished buildings have been moved and rebuilt on the 300-acre site. Many of them were moved from areas flooded by the Mactaquac Dam. Within each home, farm, and shop, costumed guides follow the rhythms of rural life. A woman, in her long, blue frock, bakes bread in the fireplace. At the ox barn one massive beast struggles against its harness while a farmer hammers on a new shoe. The site works on your imagination and sparks experiences of sights, sounds, and smells of the nineteenth century. When I entered a home and saw a family eating at the table, I felt oddly intrusive. Apologizing, I tiptoed around the house, awkwardly gawking at the furniture and hoping I wasn't disturbing their meal. The realism is magical.

Back on Highway 2, the highway rolls slightly; at some points the road sneaks down to the bank and then quickly climbs, giving majestic views over the wide, serene river. After about 16 km, you pass Drummies General Store, and after another 11.5 km you pass the road to Sunset Campground at Hawkshaw. Turn **right** after a km over the bridge at **Exit 232**, to **105**. A km farther from Highway 2, turn **right** toward Nackawic. After another 3 km you arrive at **Nackawic** (full provisions), and, if your day hasn't been exciting enough, this small town boasts the world's largest ax.

Nackawic to Muniac Provincial Park: 108.5 kilometers

Return by way of **105 North** and continue on it following the Glooscap Reach section of the river. The sticky smell of sap hangs in the air as you cycle past cottages and homes sitting on the river's slopes. The road glides beside the slow river and trips over rolling hills covered with thick forest interspersed with riverfront cottages and cattle farms. Past Nackawic 45 km, turn left over the 1.5-km bridge at **Grafton** to reach **103**. Woodstock lies 3.5 km to your left.

Woodstock is a riverside town of 5,000 where the Meduxnekeag and St. John rivers meet. Halfway between the Bay of Fundy and the St. John's headwaters, it's a place of elegant homes and shady streets. If

The author, about to enter the world's longest covered bridge at Hartland

you want to explore the town, pick up the *Woodstock Walkabout* brochure at the tourist office.

Highway 103 gives you an insight into the magnitude of the area's farming industry. The rolling hills are planted with potatoes waiting for harvest and shipment to the processing plants upriver. The hills through this area are shorter and steeper than the earlier stretch of 105. After 16.5 km, turn **right** to **105** to **Hartland**, and after 400 meters, you enter the world's longest covered bridge.

Local legends wistfully promise that your dreams will come true if you hold your breath, cross your fingers, and traverse the bridge. Good luck if you're cycling its 391-meter length. Practically speaking, an uncovered wooden bridge was expected to last only fifteen years before the planks and underpinnings rotted, but a covered bridge was expected to last up to eighty years. Horses would also be reassured, believing the bridge was a stable's entrance and calmly crossing over the rushing water. Apparently, young suitors trained their horses to stop inside the bridge so the young couple could court and kiss privately. Of the thousands of covered bridges built at the turn of the century, only a handful remain in Quebec, New England, and New Brunswick.

Immediately after crossing the bridge (use the walkway), turn **left** on **Main Street**, following **105**. At the hilltop you'll have expansive views over Hartland and the river. After 11 km, you come to **Stickney** (general store). The road is mostly flat, ambling beside the river bank until **Florenceville** springs into view.

Florenceville, once known as Buttermilk Creek but renamed in honor of Florence Nightingale, is a bustling town due to Canada's largest food processing plant. At the plant, French fries, instant mashed potatoes, hash browns, and every other conceivable processed potato product roll off the production lines.

As you leave town along 105, continue beside the river. The traffic increases until you reach **Bath** about 10 km up the road. Another 7.5 km along a ridge, after passing potato fields, nurseries, and pastureland, take you to the parking area to **Beechwood Dam** and a picnic area. The grounds display a floral clock, well-manicured gardens, and a fish elevator that lifts spawning salmon over the dam's wall. After about 9 km, along a slightly rolling road, you arrive at the beech and maple slopes of **Muniac Provincial Park**.

Muniac Provincial Park to Grand Falls: 95.1 kilometers

From the park a painless road passes along the river bank for about 14 km to **Perth-Andover**. This small town is primarily a truck stop, and although it has full provisions, it doesn't have much else to keep you there. In Perth-Andover turn right onto **109**, leaving the St. John River. The road immediately starts climbing and weaving between hills, alongside mountain streams, and beside walls of rock. The first 10 km of the road are hilly, but then it follows the main tributary of the St. John, the Tobique River. Past Highway 105 22.5 km finds you in **Arthurette** (general store). The roads around Arthurette cross endless multimillion-dollar potato farms. Notice the potato houses, half

A potato barn, flanked by earthen hills to keep the barn temperature cool, near Plaster Rock

buried to keep the potatoes naturally refrigerated and to protect them against autumn frost. Despite the sign exhorting you to turn left to Plaster Rock, stay **right** on **109**. After about 21 km along this gentle road, spiced with a couple of surprise hills, turn **right** onto the **108 West** on-ramp. To your left is the "Renous Road," an isolated 117-km stretch of road heading to Bathurst. Keep **right**, climb the bridge and hill, arriving at the junction to **Plaster Rock**. The town is to your right and the municipal park with camping is directly to your left.

From the campground at Plaster Rock stay on **108** for 4.5 km, keeping right at the junction with 390. The next section of the road becomes hilly as it passes over the Cameron Mountain Range. There is some lumbering activity in the area, so be careful of trucks storming down the road. After 21 km, you arrive in the small settlement of **New Denmark**.

The town of New Denmark is one of Canada's first Danish settlements and one of the oldest Danish communities in the world outside Denmark. As you cycle beside the road, mailboxes display names such as Hansen and Pedersen, and the white-crossed red flag of Denmark flies from many gables.

The promise of 100 acres of free land to every adult male lured the original twenty-nine settlers from Denmark. When they arrived they found thick forest instead of the sublime farmland they had been promised. Penniless and with no hope of returning home, they began clearing the trees, eventually reaping potatoes and the rewards of their hard work. This spirit and determination are celebrated during Founders' Day, when 1,000 people of Danish descent celebrate their ancestry. The Memorial Museum, about 10 km north from Hendrickson's Store, displays farming and domestic items from the settlers' lives.

The next 10 km are the hardest of the tour. The road rolls over tightly bunched, steep hills blanketed by prosperous potato fields. About 13.5 km from New Denmark, passing **Drummond**, you follow **108 West**, arriving at **Grand Falls** and the interpretive center for the falls.

The cascades drop 21 meters and rush through a 1.5-km-long gorge. The best views are from the bridge crossing the gorge. Trails lead down stairways to the gorge and potholes created by the water's fury.

TOUR NO. 12

KOOSHE AND PARLEE

Start/Finish: Chatham/Parlee Beach Provincial Park
Distance: 255 kilometers (155.5 miles)
Estimated time: 4 days, including 1 day at Kouchibouguac National Park
Terrain: Flat
Map: New Brunswick Travel Map
Connecting tours: Tour Nos. 5, 11, 14, 15, 16, 17, 18, 19
Connections: Highways 15 and 8

As you cycle along the Acadian coast friendly locals may greet you with the Franglais phrase, "Hi! Ça va?" You'll see signs advertising foods such as *hommard frais, poutine râpée,* and *coques frites.* You'll find laissez-faire people helpful to strangers but passionately defending their identify and beliefs. You'll find Acadia.

This section of the Acadian coast represents a culture distinct from most others found in the Maritimes, and it's on New Brunswick's northeast coast that this special culture is strongest.

Kouchibouguac (pronounced *koosh-e-boo-quack*) National Park is a unique area of natural history. Snuggled along the Gulf of St. Lawrence coast, the park is a captivating combination of forests, bogs, salt marshes, and barrier islands. They blend like a curry, each habitat mixing to produce an intricate, singular ecosystem. Although lacking the spectacular grandeur of the Rocky Mountains or the tortuous wonder of the Cabot Trail, Kouchibouguac is a fascinating study of a complex and unique ecosystem. The park's bike trails allow easy exploration of the park.

Supplies are easily available except in Kouchibouguac. Bike shops are only in Moncton and Newcastle, both off the tour's route. There is bike rental available at Kouchibouguac. You should find the climate comfortable; winds blow from the southwest and the northwest. Always carry insect repellent with you.

The tour along the Acadian coast is a gem. Tracing the shore, devoid of traffic, the route passes weathered fishing villages, home towns of intriguing characters, and relaxed beach resorts—each spiced with Acadian joie de vivre.

Chatham to Kouchibouguac National Park: 112 kilometers

Chatham, Newcastle, Douglastown, and Nelson-Miramichi form an industrial center at the mouth of the Miramichi River. Straddling the

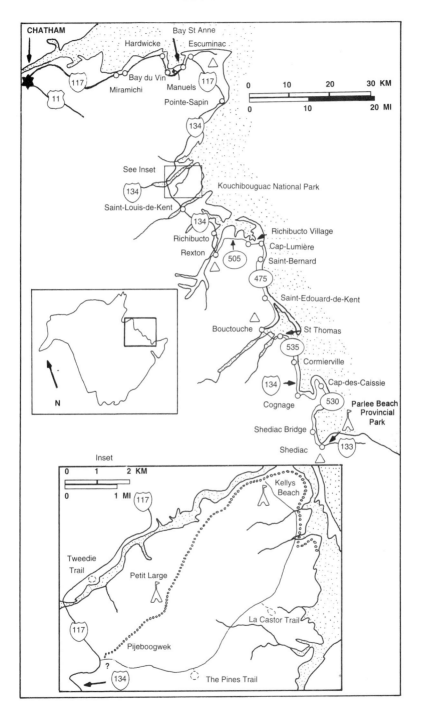

river is the **Highway 11 bridge**, the tour's start. At the bridge's foot take the exit **east** toward Chatham's center. After 100 meters, turn **left** onto **Church Avenue** and then make the first **right** onto **Wellington Street**. The scant downtown area lies two blocks to the left. After 600 meters, at the corner of University Avenue, you pass the small Chatham Museum. Wellington Street (**Highway 117**) carries you out of town. After a couple of kilometers, you find yourself between walls of trees lined with houses tucked into the woods. Shortly after the exit for Loggieville, the flat road angles inland to the right, continuing through thick second-growth forest. Unfortunately, some of this tour's roads have been battered by overweight trucks. As the road continues, it passes open pasture and hayfields. Noticing Black River to your left, after 28 km, you pass the village of **Miramichi** (no provisions) and the attractive **Bay du Vin**. Traffic from local peat moss cultivation may increase through this section. In another 3 km you pass the small lobster fishing port of **Bay du Vin**.

Along this road you'll notice exuberant wildflowers growing in the water-filled ditches. Showy blue flag irises, white-hooded jack-in-the-pulpits, small-pouched lady slippers, and the widespread pink and purple lupines help pass the time on the next section. Over the next 11 km, you pass three exits for Hardwicke until you arrive at **Manuels** about 3 km from the last Hardwicke exit. Manuels has a convenience store, but if you need food wait until **Bay St. Anne** 2 km farther since it has a more substantial grocery.

As you cycle along the 6-km stretch of town Acadian flags flap in front of neat homes. About 8 km past the center of Bay St. Anne, you pass through **Escuminac** and come to the left junction with the continuation of **117**. If you follow Escuminac Point Road straight ahead, after about 2 km you come to a stoic monument, designed by Claude Roussel, commemorating the 35 fishermen who lost their lives in the 1959 Escuminac disaster.

Another km takes you to **Escuminac Beach**, a pleasant day park with dune and beach access. Back along **117**, after you pass the small homes, you come across lonely stretches of birch forest and wetlands. Watch for the peat moss plant 7 km farther. After another 10 km along a ragged road, bordered by open marsh and spruce forest, you arrive at **Pointe-Sapin**. This active little town has the last grocery store between here and Saint-Louis-de-Kent. From Pointe-Sapin, it's 7.5 km to the Kouchibouguac National Park boundary. Only a sign and the well-maintained road mark your passage into the park. As most travelers arrive from the south and just visit the beach, park officials feel there's no need for a map or information booth at the northern boundary. Anyway, you'll appreciate the well-manicured ditches and forest as you cycle along the delightful road. In 13 km from the entrance, you come to the **Claire-Fontaine Trail**, the first of the park's hiking trails. This 3.4-km hike winds through the birch forest and follows the banks of the Claire Fontaine River. About 2.5 km farther, you pass **Tweedie Trail**, a fifteen-minute walk over a boardwalk that traverses a river marsh. The Park Administration Office is 3.5 km from the trail. Turn left and then right to the **Park Administration Office** so you

The monument to the survivors of the Escuminac disaster

can register for the primitive campground and gather any other information you need.

The bicycle trails in the park are not well marked. If you intend to stay at the main campground, follow the 12.5-km road that leads to it. About 50 meters from the park office junction, following the sign for

Pijeboogwek, turn **left** past the bicycling gate. After 100 meters, turn **right** past the parking lot. Crushed gravel covers the bike trail so it's easily passable for most bikes. After 2.5 km, at **Petit Large Rest Area**, keep **right**, and after another 700 meters you reach **Petit Large**, the primitive campground with a water pump, dry toilets, and a supply of firewood. The campground is accessible only by bike and foot. So, even though at the main campground there may be a perpetual lineup for the trailers, campers, and recreational vehicles, you'll be able to cycle up to a quiet, unfrequented campground and stay for a fraction of the price. The only disadvantage is that you have to cycle the 6.5 km up to the main campground to shower and to do laundry.

KOUCHIBOUGUAC NATIONAL PARK

Kouchibouguac National Park is not majestic and awe-inspiring. No sparkling lakes mirror the reflections of snow-capped mountains, and no breathtaking deserts spread out to the horizons to glow in a magnificent sunset. Instead, you have to take the time to observe and inspect the park's multilayered, intricate ecosystems.

Each habitat has its unique character, but each is a part of the environmental blend. The ever-shifting dune system is over 3,500 years old. At Kelly's Beach a floating boardwalk crosses the lagoons to reach the popular beaches on the windward side of the dunes. The boardwalk also protects the fragile anchoring system of Marram grass and false heather grass. Dunes provide a shelter for carnivorous pitcher plants and sundews and a nesting area for savannah and sharp-tailed sparrows that feed on the abundant mosquito, fly, and katydid populations. The warm-water lagoons separate the dunes from the mainland. Fed by streams and rivers, the freshwater mingles with the saltwater from the shifting tides, allowing verdant eel grass, rock crabs, starfish, squid, and snails that can withstand the ever-changing degrees of salt to flourish. Visit the Tweedie, Osprey, and Salt Marsh trails to view this particular habitat. Inland bogs comprise 21 percent of the park's total area. Underlain by a clay so dense water can't seep through, the terrain combines with the cool, humid climate to produce these spongy bogs. Despite the proportion of bog in the park, only the Bog Trail provides an example of a dome of sphagnum moss 4,500 years old and 6 meters deep. In areas where the land is more porous, the forests were cleared for grazing and crops by the Acadians and United Empire Loyalists. Today the white pine, red spruce, and paper birch are beginning to return to a more natural state. The Cedar and Pines Trail allows you to explore some of the old-growth forest and examine the rebirth of the forest habitat.

Kouchibouguac National Park is unique for its system of bike trails. You could easily spend the day traveling over 20 km of bike trails and stopping to explore all eleven hiking trails, ranging in hiking time from 20 minutes to 3 hours. Most of the trails are well maintained and have interpretive signs so you can appreciate and learn about each habitat. Raised boardwalks cross the streams and sections of soggy ground.

Spend the day exploring the trails, swimming in the lagoons, and cycling beside the Kouchibouguac River.

Kouchibouguac National Park Campground Entrance to Bouctouche: 80 kilometers

From the campground entrance leave the administration office and after 200 meters turn **left** onto the park road. After less than 6 km you come to the **La Castor Trail**.

This quick 1.4-km trail circles the habitat once created by a beaver family. The influence of these small mammals, Canada's national animal, is dramatic. Once they finish a dam the resulting flood suffocates and kills the surrounding trees. Water-resistant species such as alder begin to take over, attracting new birds, such as warblers, redstarts, and yellowthroats.

Along the park road about 3 km farther, you arrive at another trail, **The Pines**. This 800-meter, 25-minute walk meanders into a rare mature section of the Acadian forest. The commanding white pines that survived the last century of logging and the Miramichi Fire of 1825 dominate the area.

About 3.5 km from the trail, you arrive back at the Park Administration building. After 200 meters, turn **left** back onto **117 South**, and after about 1.5 km, turn **left** onto **134 South**. Within 1 km you pass a restaurant, grocery store, campground, motel, and frivolous amusements. Within 5 km you come to **Saint-Louis-de-Kent** (supermarket). Look for the province's most elaborate shrine modeled after Notre Dame at Lourdes. From this village you pass over 11 km of drab riding to come to **Richibucto**. The town's biggest site is the modern St. Louis of Aloysius Catholic Church. The contoured roof is supposed to represent ocean waves and the bell tower a lighthouse. Avoiding the business section of town, immediately after the church turn right on Acadie Street. After about 5.5 km, passing under busy Highway 11, you reach **Rexton** and **Bonar Law Avenue** (116 West).

Bonar Law Historic Park lies 0.5 km to the right. Open from July to August, this 9-hectare park nestled on the river bank gives you an idea of how the rural middle class lived at the turn of the century. The park commemorates the birthplace of Andrew Bonar Law, Britain's only foreign-born prime minister. Elected in 1922 he died only a year later, but his rise from humble beginnings to one of the most powerful positions in the world is impressive.

Continuing on **134 South** for another 0.5 km, you arrive in downtown **Rexton** and in another km turn **left** on **Centennial Avenue** (**505 South**). This quiet road passes through more Acadian forests for more than 11 km until you pass through **Richibucto Village**. After another 3.5 km turn **right** at **Cap-Lumière**, continuing on **505**. The road follows the coast with impressive views of the Northumberland Strait, windswept sand cliffs, and small cattle farms. At 7 km continue **left**, and after another 3.3 km jog **left** again onto **Saint-Anne Shore Road**. After 2 km, you come to the rustic fishing settlement of

Saint-Bernard (no provisions), and after another 2 km turn **left** onto **475 South**. The road now follows a built-up area of cottages and settlements, including **Saint-Edouard-de-Kent**, after 3 more km. In another 2 km you pass the beach with a nesting area for the endangered piping plover, of which only 240 nesting pairs survive. Because of the need for protection, beach access is prohibited from May 15 to August 1. After 9.5 km, you pass the shoreline, cluttered with houses and driveways, to land in the popular resort and oyster bed of New Brunswick, **Bouctouche**.

Bouctouche is derived from Micmac, meaning "little big harbor." Five Acadian families, returning from exile in 1784, founded the village, which now has a population of around 2,400. The dominant Acadian heritage has inspired many artists, the most famous being Antoinine Maillet. Describing and commenting on the Acadian political and social scene, Ms. Maillet has become an international spokesperson for her culture. Her most famous novel, *La Sagouine*, is based on the character of a washerwoman whose down-to-earth monologue has been re-created by actress Viola Léger. Ms. Léger has taken the experiences of the indomitable heroine to stages around the world, including a theme park, La Pays de la Sagouine. The country of la Sagouine is an island linked by a 305-meter bridge and is a stage for actors impersonating the characters from Ms. Maillet's literature. Orations, concerts, and supper theaters are also held here during the tourist season.

Throughout the Maritimes, every tourist will pass "Irving" gas stations, "Irving" forestry lots, and "Irving" shipbuilding yards. The Irving insignia is everywhere. In the early 1920s K.C. Irving began building his conglomerate here, at his small gas station. Determined to become a success, he would get up from his bed above the station at any hour to pump gas for a customer. His hard-nosed manner fueled an empire that grew to include gas refineries, forestry products, agriculture, and any resource-based industry that would make his family money. He was a whirlwind economic power. Today, his three sons and one daughter own one of the richest corporations in North America, including sawmills, newspapers, and television stations. Every local has something to say about the Irvings.

A last sight to see in Bouctouche is the **Kent Museum**. Occupying a convent and school built in 1880, the Kent Society converted it to a museum depicting Acadian art and a neo-Gothic chapel created by Léon Léger, "the one who made wood pray."

Bouctouche to Shediac: 63 kilometers

In Bouctouche return **left** on **134 South** over the bridge. On the other side of the river is the entrance to La Pays de la Sagouine. Past Highway 475 3 km, after the second bridge, turn **left** on **535 South**. The road follows a pleasant shore drive with houses beautifully set on small protruding spits of land. Across the small bay you can see the Dune de Bouctouche and its lighthouse sentinel. The next small villages of **St. Thomas** and **Cormierville** both have convenience stores. After 18.5 km turn **left** at **Cognage** onto **530**. Nicholas Denys, one of

The author poses by the "world's largest lobster," which greets visitors to Shediac.

the founding French settlers of New Brunswick, called the town Utopia when a storm forced him to take shelter in the harbor and he found everything to keep him comfortable. After less than a km, turn **left** onto **530**. The first portion of this road is boring, but as you turn the cape you come to **Cap-des-Caissie** with its long sheltered beaches, campgrounds, and convenience stores. Locals and those wanting to avoid the hubbub of Shediac use these more secluded beaches. After 11 km keep **left** again, and after another 2.5 km turn **left** on **134 South**. A km later you pass the village of **Shediac Bridge**. The road crosses a one-lane bridge that yields to oncoming traffic, so be careful. After 5 km continue straight for **133 East**. After 1.5 km turn left, continuing on 133. This route is busy, particularly on summer weekends. Don't miss the world's largest lobster welcoming you into the town of **Shediac**, the world's lobster capital. From the lobster it's 4.8 km to the **left** turn to **Parlee Beach Provincial Park**, which lies another 1.6 km down the road.

Shediac is bustling with clubs, cafes, and restaurants. Its warm water, fine sand beaches, restaurants, and accommodations act as a resort for the population of Moncton and other travelers heading to or returning from Prince Edward Island. The town is a perfect spot to celebrate the end of the tour; revel over a lobster supper, and reminisce about this remarkable route.

PRINCE EDWARD ISLAND

INTRODUCTION

Geography

Prince Edward Island (PEI) is Canada's smallest and most densely populated province. Looking at the tourism department's highway map, you'll find the distances are beguiling. Just 273 km will take you across the province from North Cape to East Point; 30 km will take you across the island's central width. However, cycling along the island's rolling roads, passing by the ordered potato fields, you'll notice little land remains unused. Unlike other Canadian provinces, almost every patch of its 5,678 square km is being utilized by man, and only the poorly drained parts of the island, the bogs and marshes, have been left to the wilds. The 130,000 people who live on the island use

An array of "Anne" dolls in a shop window in Cavendish

Charlottetown (population 15,400) and Summerside (7,500) as their business centers. The rest of the inhabitants are like dandelion seeds scattered in the wind, left to seed and take root on family farms; others have scattered to other industrialized provinces to look for homes.

Most cyclists arriving on the island expect level roads; after all, such a small island can't be rigorous. But when they start hitting the hills of the interior and the rolling coastline of the west shore, they realize cycling through the island involves some effort.

The island is known as "Canada's Million-Acre Farm" and the "Garden in the Gulf." Everyone keeps their fields and lawns neatly manicured. The rusty soil on the farms becomes golden sand on the beaches. Dunes rise as high as 18 meters, anchored by sturdy Marram grass.

The island's economy relies on primary resources. The rolling farmland constitutes the majority of PEI's land, and agriculture ranks second behind tourism as an economic mainstay; crop success affects every inhabitant. Forestry disappeared long ago; shipbuilding in the 1800s devastated the once expansive woodlands. The sea offers rewards such as Irish moss, lobsters, mussels, and oysters. The industrial base remains small, and the reliance on primary resources and tourism has created problems.

The island hosts 700,000 tourists a year, almost six times the number of inhabitants. This seasonal invasion threatens the reasons the tourists were lured in the first place—quiet idyllic countryside and people who embrace conservative values. The inhabitants find themselves in a quandary: either to maintain a way of life (heavily subsidized by the federal government) based on farming, fishing, and seasonal jobs for the tourist industry, or to industrialize and expand the tourist infrastructure to enter the quickly pulsing global economy surrounding them. Recently, the provincial government rejected a plan to enter into a partnership with New Brunswick to build the Point Lepreau Nuclear Generating Station, and the locals rebuffed the advances of a military defense contract. However, the tide may be turning. In the summer of 1993, after intensive debate, the government began construction of a fixed link (islanders refuse to call it a bridge) to connect Prince Edward Island to the rest of Canada.

History

After the last Ice Age, 11,000 years ago, Paleo-Indians inhabited the region. Then the land mass was still part of New Brunswick, but with the land rising and the glaciers melting, it became an island. Before the Europeans arrived, Micmacs were regular visitors to the island. Around the shorelines, archaeologists have unearthed ancient campsites, identified by shell middens (large heaps of seashells dumped by the encamped aboriginal people). *Abegweit*, "land cradled on the waves," offered a pleasing stopover for a summer of hunting and fishing.

The first European to see the island was Jacques Cartier, who in 1534, described it as "low and most beautiful to see." At the time, thick mantles of spruce and fir trees cloaked the island. Sixty years later, a private French venture brought the first settlers to Isle St. Jean, but they were unprepared for the difficult work of clearing the land of boulders. Because they had to use trial and error to devise new agricultural techniques, the disastrous years outnumbered the prosperous ones. The enterprise went bankrupt, and all but a few settlers returned to France. The French at Louisbourg, an artificial city designed to protect France's holdings in North America, was without a food base, so they devised a plan to use Isle St. Jean to supply food for the fortress. French officials tried to entice and strong-arm the Acadians in Nova Scotia to resettle. Only a few settlers came, farming around Port La Joye (now near Charlottetown).The farming remained difficult. Drought, fire, plagues of locusts, and field mice were the hardships that kept the settlers hungry. However, when the British deported the mainland Acadians in 1755, the island population soared from 650 to 5,000. Unprepared and ill-equipped, the refugees arriving on the island were pitiable. Father Girard, a local parish priest, described them: "They cannot protect themselves from the cold either by day or night. Most of the children are so naked that they cannot cover themselves when I enter their huts and find them sitting in the ashes beside the fire. . . ."

In July 1758, Louisbourg fell to the British for the last time and 500 soldiers arrived on the island to evacuate the inhabitants to France, a land most Acadians had never seen. Evading the British, thirty families hid in the forests and isolated coves. They struggled and stayed, eventually forming the nucleus of the Acadian culture still found on the island.

Shortly afterward, the British government implemented a lottery to distribute St. John Island. The lottery, based on Captain Samuel Holland's precise survey of the island, would have repercussions for 200 years. The lottery was fixed so influential merchants, speculators, and bureaucrats received the sixty available lots. As conditions of ownership, the landowners were to provide for Protestant settlers, to develop the lots, and to pay rent on the property. Many, hoping for a quick profit, ignored all the conditions. Land became power, a condition that continues to the present day.

From the late 1700s, politics dominated the island's development. Landowners controlled their lots as fiefdoms, and despite some earnest attempts, it was the British government, influenced by absentee landowners, that wielded control. After almost 100 years, land reform became essential—too much power was held by a few landowners and politicians who mollified any changes to their benefit. Populist uprisings, political scandals, and an elected legislature finally moved the British government to buy the land from the landlords and offer to sell it to the tenants.

Islanders began dreaming of greatness, and they began to build what they thought was the key to the island's success—a railway. However, haunted by greed and corruption, the scheme turned into a nightmare. Every community wanted to be connected to the line, and the company that won the contract specified a cost per mile of track and not how many miles would be built. So the rail line meandered needlessly through the countryside, the train stopping at a station every 3 miles. Money was burned like coal in the belly of a locomotive. The provincial debt soared from $250,000 to over $4 million. Lenders demanded their money, and Canada promised to help them reduce their debt load if they joined the Confederation. John A. Macdonald, Canada's prime minister then, desperately wanted PEI to join before the United States, deeply engrossed in civil war, invaded the island. Resentfully, on July 1, 1873, Prince Edward Island became a province of Canada, a decision still discussed by islanders.

The late 1800s were the island's golden age. Shipbuilding, the main industry, brought enormous wealth to the island. White spruce for masts, shallow harbors for launching, and the proximity to world markets made the island an ideal building center. Newly built ships, loaded with lumber and fish, sailed to England and the West Indies and were then sold. Between 1830 and 1873, over 3,000 ships were launched into the gulf waters. The builders quickly depleted the forests, and the arrival of steam and steel closed this golden age. By the end of the century, the island had become a small backwater, propped by federal grants. Today, tourism and agriculture are the dominant economic factors, and internal debates rage over keeping the "island way" or succumbing to the vagaries of people from "away."

Weather

You can begin cycling on the island as early as May, when average daytime temperatures hover around 14 degrees Celsius. However, overnight temperatures can drop to 4 degrees, and May can see heavy rains. As the spring dances into summer, the cycling conditions slip into perfection—bright summer days and moderate temperatures restrained by west and southwest breezes. The biggest problem you may face is traffic, but most of the tourists concentrate around Charlottetown and Cavendish. As the summer sneaks into autumn, leaves ignite into small flames of color and farmers hastily harvest their crops. Tourists vacate the island and the islanders relax. September and October are beautiful months to explore the land and learn about the people.

Accommodations and Supplies

Since the island sees so many tourists, you might expect extensive tourist facilities—don't. Most tourists converge around Cavendish's beaches where the facilities thrive. The west and east coasts remain isolated and quiet areas where finding accommodations is hit and miss. Although provincial park campgrounds lie sprinkled around the island, tourists place heavy demands on them during the summer. You'll want to reserve a place to stay. Luckily, there the "Dial-the-Island" information and reservation system is available for registered accommodations and provincial parks. Check with tourist information

One of the cannons of Fort Amherst overlooks the entrance to Charlottetown Harbor.

for the current toll-free number. As in all provinces, you cannot reserve sites in national parks.

Ever since 1866 when the first horseless carriages scared the bejeezus out of islanders, automobiles have affected the island way of life. One of the recent casualties of the assault has been the general store. Today, no part of the island is more than an hour by car from Charlottetown's and Summerside's supermarkets and food warehouses. As a result, the sporadic, minuscule transactions generated by small family-run stores aren't worth the owner's investment, so many are boarded up and forgotten. When you're cycling keep stocked with food and you'll have a great trip.

TOUR NO. 13

UP WEST

Start/Finish:	Jacques Cartier Provincial Park/ Jacques Cartier Provincial Park
Distance:	143.5 kilometers (87.5 miles)
Estimated time:	2 days
Terrain:	Flat to slightly hilly
Map:	Prince Edward Island Highway Map
Connecting tours:	Tour No. 14
Connections:	Highway 2

This tour travels through PEI's most remote area. Islanders prejudicially refer to it as "up west," hillbilly country—where the uncouth, uneducated, and unfriendly locals don't want to have anything to do with people from "away." Yet during Prince County's history, fox breeders became the richest men on the island and Stompin' Tom Connors grew up here to become a Canadian cultural icon. One of Canada's largest wooden tracker-action organs is still used for classical recitals here. Yet history and friendly people are only part of the area's allure. The seacoast dominates. At Jacques Cartier Provincial Park the sea paints the shores, farther north serrated headlands slice the surf, and along the western coast free winds rush excitedly over the sea and land.

Supplies are difficult to find en route. The most reliable are at Tignish, Miminegash, West Point, and Alberton. The island's only bike shop is in Charlottetown. You'll find a temperate climate with prevailing winds blowing from the west and southwest.

The land embraces farming. Rows of potato plants bounce along the hills of red earth. The cattle nuzzle grassy blankets tucked in under the cliffs. A sense of peace and solitude spreads over the landscape's soul. Farmers still wave from their tractors and storekeepers still complain about the weather—even if you are from "away."

Jacques Cartier Provincial Park to Cedar Dunes Provincial Park: 43.4 kilometers

The fully serviced Jacques Cartier Provincial Park swoons by the sea. Its beachfront encourages musings and meditation. From the park head south along **Highway 12**. About 5 km from the park, you come to an unpaved road announcing the direction for the Prince Edward Island Miniature Railway (PEIMR).

From the miniature railway's junction travel 3.5 km to **Alberton**,

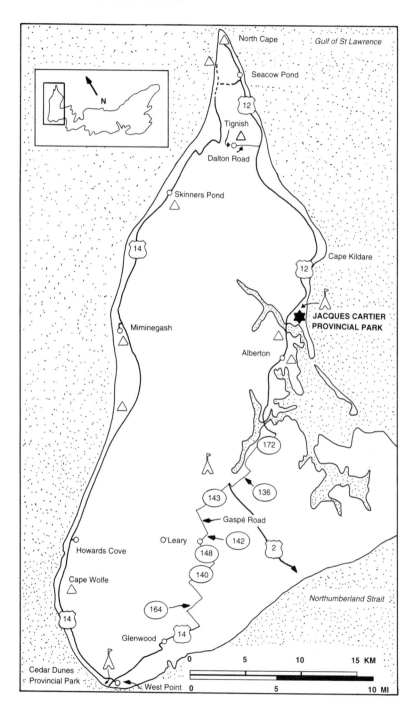

once the richest town in PEI thanks to a small black canid. Throughout the area, "fox mansions" dot the towns and hamlets, vestiges of the fortunes of the silver fox industry. You can learn more about the area's heritage and fox industry and tour the jail and courthouse at Alberton Museum only 300 meters past the town's main intersection along Highway 12.

Past the museum 700 meters, keep **left** following **Highway 12**. About 6 km farther, passing flat agricultural land, and after crossing Mill River, turn **right** on **172**. The road rises onto a ridge overlooking the river and veers right along the boundary for Mill River Provincial Park. The road ends after 4 km at **136**, where you turn **right**. The entrance to the park and campground comes upon you after 1.5 km, and a few hundred meters farther you come to Highway 2. The route begins to zigzag between potato field lots, grazing cattle, and farmhouses. At **Highway 2**, turn **right** and take the next **left**, only 100 meters farther at the church following **143**. Stay on this rolling road for 4 km until you take the first paved left along **Gaspé Road**. About 2.5 km **south**, you come to **O'Leary**. This bustling little town serves as a commercial area for the southwestern farmers and fishers. At the end of this road turn **right** on **142** and you're downtown. A km through town, turn **right** on **148**. If you want to visit Canada's only potato museum, stay on 142 to Parkview Drive and turn right.

Potatoes are king on Spud Island. The crop's success affects every islander. Only the tourist industry is bigger. The first carload of potatoes on PEI arrived in 1918, and the farmers of Lot 16, just south of O'Leary, developed the tubers. Today, the island's potatoes are sent to the United States, South America, Italy, Africa, and the Caribbean.

The route deflects and bounces, following old lot markings and farmers' fields. Patches of woods spring up where the ground is too wet for farming. Highway 148 ends after 2 km, where you turn **right** on **140**. The road zigzags, veering **left**, then **right**, then **left** over 6 km. Follow the signs for 140 until you come to the junction for **164 South**. Turn **left** for 2 km then turn **right** on **14**. With that little complicated maze out of the way, stay on 14 as the road begins to veer toward the sea. Keep your eyes open for the tractor-operated sawmill to the right. Keep **left** at the fork for 139 at Glenwood, and 9.5 km farther is the junction for West Point. If you need provisions before heading to the park, the village, 500 meters to the right, has a small grocery and a dirt road leading to the park. Otherwise, the park entrance is 800 meters farther along 14. At the park junction turn **left** and visit **Cedar Dunes Provincial Park**.

Cedar Dunes Provincial Park to Jacques Cartier Provincial Park: 100.1 kilometers

The unique thing, probably in all of Canada, about Cedar Dunes is the black-and-white-striped lighthouse rising out of the red sand to puncture the blue sky. On the first floor of the lighthouse is a small museum displaying artifacts and photographs of the museum since its

1875 inception. The second floor is the keeper's quarters, and the third floor is reserved for overnight travelers. On the lighthouse's pinnacle, the electronic beacon guides freighters and oil tankers around the cape. The park also offers a campground and a rust-colored beach stretching for almost 2 km. Before you begin your day, make sure you have enough provisions to last to Tignish or at least Miminegash. Provisions are difficult to find.

Mobility has its price, and part of that price has been the demise of the local general store. You'll find little tourist activity on this isolated shore; closed canteens, boarded-up restaurants, and shriveled gas stations mark the passage of time. Remember the words of Anne of Avonlea: "I think an old deserted house is such a sad sight. . . . It always seems to me to be thinking about its past and mourning for its old time joys."

Beginning your day, cycle westward toward the shore. As you pass the final section of swamp and trees, the shore stretches out to welcome you. From here, the road begins to rise and dip over a treeless landscape of pastures reaching to the cliff sides and potato fields rolling beside the road. Headlands, capes, and cliffs, sculpted by the winds, surrender to the sea. The detritus crumbles into the water to create a murky sea, but beyond the tide line, the clear ocean swells to the horizon.

After about 8 km, stop and admire the view of **Carey Point** behind you. Less than 3.5 km farther you pass **Cape Wolfe**, the landing area for General James Wolfe. The general reputedly landed here before he conquered Quebec and crushed the French empire in Canada. Down the road another 2.5 km you find the turn for **Howards Cove**, which is worth a look. Lobster and clam boats moor at the docks of this classic harbor. On top of the squat red cliffs sits the squat red-and-white lighthouse. Visit the fishing crews and see how the catch has been.

Continuing on Highway 14, 13 km farther north is **Campbellton Provincial Park**, offering a tranquil spot to stop, rest, and meditate. Beyond the park the road begins to veer inland, rolling through isolated forest to avoid Little Miminegash Pond. You arrive at the village of **Miminegash** after 10 km. This small fishing village has a small unpredictable grocery where you can stock up on food.

From town, following **Highway 14**, you'll usually be within sight of the ocean, regimented rows of potato fields, and a big bowl of blue sky. The road also calms down, slipping along flat plains and small hills. In another 13 km you come to **Skinners Pond**. This little village looks like only a speck on the plain, but it was here that one of Canada's cultural icons grew up. Stompin' Tom Connors, country-and-western legend, composer of thirty-seven albums—including the songs *Hockey Night in Canada* and *Bud the Spud* (yes, *that* Bud the Spud)—grew up and went to school in this isolated little spot. Today, you can visit the schoolhouse museum, containing paraphernalia and souvenirs of Stompin' Tom.

In another 7 km the road makes a weird left turn, but stay on 14, which eventually skips into gravel. No need to worry though, as the

road is kept in good shape and is no worse than sections of paved Highway 12 ahead. The road veers right after 5.2 km, but a smaller,
rougher dirt road continues straight, heading to Elephant Rock, 1.5 km
farther. The side road, skirting the cliff side, deteriorates into a small
two-wheeled path, filled in with gravel and rocks. You find a parking
area, but if you've made it this far by riding, you can continue to the
rock. This enormous sea stack, amazingly, looks like a standing elephant with its trunk dipping into the salty water. In a few years, the
appeal of this curiosity will be lost. Apparently, the trunk is eroding
and will soon collapse.

Back on the main route, the gravel and Highway 14 end at the village of **Seacow Pond**. Turn **left** on **12**. As you cycle along this wind-
whipped coast you pass the menacing Black Marsh. Bleached and
burnt skeletal remains of hawthorn bushes surround this large bog.
Also watch for the large draft horses grazing in the fields. These hefty
beasts have made a comeback since the revitalization of the Irish moss
industry. In the past, harvesters waited for a storm to dislodge the
moss, but now they use the horses and a metal dredge to collect it.

After nearly 4 km, you arrive at **North Cape**, the windiest spot on

Two visitors walk along the shore near Elephant Rock.

Prince Edward Island. The Atlantic Wind Test Site proves it. The site operates as an international laboratory for the study and development of wind energy. Watch the different sails and blades pirouette and whirl in the wind. The meeting of the winds and tides of the Gulf of St. Lawrence and Northumberland Strait create an average wind speed of 14 knots. The Wind Test Site monitors the efficiency of its own turbines and others around Canada.

Return along 12, passing by **Seacow Pond**, named for the hundreds of walruses that inhabited the shore until early settlers decimated the population. Passing by the junction for 14, follow the barren shore for 9 km until you come to **Dalton Road**. Turn **right** and 1.5 km farther you're in **Tignish**, commercial and fishing center for northern Prince County. Tignish, population 900, will seem huge after your west-coast trek. Tignish has always relied on fishing. In 1923, the Tignish Fishermen's Cooperative was founded, and now the port has the largest number of tuna catches on PEI and is the world's largest producer of processed lobster products.

Before you leave town, visit the grand church of St. Simon and St. Jude, just a few hundred meters north on the main street (Highway 153). This towering brick building houses Canada's largest wooden tracker-action organ. Built in 1882, the organ is still used for recitals during the summer.

Return to 12 as it edges closer to the sea. The road, flanked by trees, winds along farms, woods, and marshes. Look for graceful blue heron and gawky cormorants in the ponds. Past the junction 9.5 km you come to a small unmarked break in the trees. Just off the side of the road is a small clearing, beckoning with views of **Cape Kildare**. These saw-toothed headlands, cutting the waves as they arrive from parts unknown, make a perfect spot to reflect on your journey. In another 4.5 km you're back at **Jacques Cartier Provincial Park**.

TOUR NO. 14

THE FRENCH SHORE

Start / Finish: Miscouche/Miscouche
Distance: 53.2 kilometers (32 miles)
Estimated time: 1 day
Terrain: Flat to slightly rolling
Map: Prince Edward Island Highway Map
Connecting tours: Tour Nos. 13 and 15
Connections: Highway 2

The flat terrain, combined with attractions and light traffic, makes for a lazy day of riding. You'll experience a parish filled with strong influences. The tricolored flags flying fiercely from farmhouses, co-ops, convents, and churches identify the area as strongly Acadian.

The French Shore region covers only about 88 square kilometers, and within this small area 95 percent of the 2,500-person population speaks French. The French Shore's lingua franca is a unique ethnic dialect nurtured through strong identity and isolation. I was speaking to the guide at the tourist office, asking about the hardiness of the Acadian language. "It's so embarrassing," she replied. "I was speaking to a man from France—a real Frenchman. I could hardly understand what he was saying and I was afraid he would think I was stupid; I wasn't speaking 'real' French." Luckily, most Acadians on PEI are bilingual, so you should have no problem communicating.

Supplies are available at Wellington and Miscouche. The winds blow from the southwest and west, and summer temperatures are usually moderate.

Miscouche to Miscouche: 53.2 kilometers

The tour begins at the **Miscouche Acadian Museum**, 100 meters east of the intersection of Highways 12 and 2. To gain an appreciation of the Acadians' story and a respect for their heritage, visit the museum. The large building, flying the red, white, and blue Acadian flag adopted at the second National Acadian Convention in 1884, documents Acadian history and displays tools, furniture, and dioramas. Most interesting are the portraits of the thirty families that went into hiding after the deportation to avoid further recrimination. Looking into their eyes, you can imagine their tales of tenacity and grit as they outwitted and hid from the British. To the Acadians, their homeland was their sea, innocence, and blood, represented in the flag's colors. Today, most of the island's Acadians are descendants of these courageous settlers.

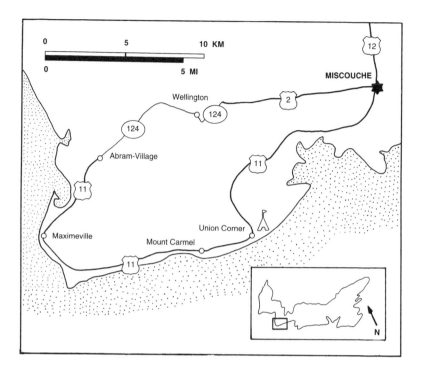

Head **west**, away from **Charlottetown**, along **2**. After only 100
meters, at the intersection with 12, pass St. John the Baptist Church.
The elaborate twin spires of the church tower above town, and the
church is worth stopping at for a look. The monolithic façade betrays
the interior's delicacy. Follow wide-shouldered **2**, rolling slightly past
farmland and crossing a marsh called Long Swamp. After 11 km, you
come to the intersection with **124**. Carefully turn **left** toward **Wellington**, which you will come to in almost 2 km. Wellington doesn't have
much to offer, being mostly a supply station for the surrounding area.
At Wellington, turn **right**, following **124**, and 400 meters farther continue **left** at a confusing intersection as the road's name changes from
Riverside Drive to **Sunset Drive**. As you leave town you have to
climb one of the few hills of the day, and at the next junction, after
2.2 km, turn **left**, staying on **124**. The road continues its gentle climb
to the top of the second hill, where the radio tower marks the tour's
highest point. You're now deep in Acadian country. Names such as
Arsenault and Gallant are spelled out on mailboxes, exuberant blues,
yellows, and reds paint the houses, and farmers still use the great, old
barns to store hay and house cattle. Soon, you see Egmont Bay tempting you forward as you drop from the hill. After about 5 km from the
previous corner, **124** ends and changes to **11** at **Abram-Village**, named
for Abraham Arsenault, the area's first French settler. Continue

A crumbling building in a deserted field near Cap-Egmont

straight to follow the tour. To your left is the Handicraft Co-op, displaying locally made crafts. Highway 11 drops to the sea. Before you cross a bridge notice the busy Acadian Fishing Co-op wharf to your right. As you pass the headland and the small hamlet of **Maximeville**, notice Cape-Egmont Lighthouse signaling in the distance. The shores along this section offer some of the more secluded beaches on the island. Backed by red sandstone cliffs you can swim, sunbathe, or search for the rumored buried treasure. The road veers eastward as you round the lighthouse, and about 10 km from Abrams-Village you come to one of the cornier attractions of the island, the **Bottle Houses**. If you can stand to part with a few dollars, you can be enthralled by the chapel and house made from more than 25,000 bottles. Admittedly, the rock gardens may have more interest. About 3 km from the Bottle Houses you come to a more interesting exhibition, **Le Village**. Since you are almost halfway through the tour you could stop at the restaurant and have a traditional Acadian meal. Repast on *poutines á trou* (pastry stuffed with fruit and covered in sugar sauce), *pâté* (meat pie), and others. Le Village, reduced to empty buildings, hasn't been the boom the parishioners hoped for, but you can spend an interesting hour here.

Refueled, after 2.5 km, at **Mount Carmel**, you pass the symmetrical church of Notre Dame, perched on the hill overlooking the sea. In 1812 a few Acadian families left the north coast and founded Mount Carmel parish. Today the convent and church stand as the parish's center-pieces. If the meal at Le Village is still weighing you down, you can rest at **Union Corner Provincial Park**, 3 km from Mount Carmel. The park, just off to the right, has a surprisingly warm beach to wade into. From Union Corner the road veers inland and you say goodbye to the sea for the remainder of the tour. The route crosses through a mixture of marsh, forest, and farmland for about 13 km until you turn **left** onto **11**. **Miscouche** beckons as you cycle the last 1.5 km back to **2** and the Notre Dame Church. The Acadian Museum is back to your right.

TOUR NO. 15

HERITAGE ROAD TOUR

Start / Finish: Victoria/Victoria
Distance: 70.2 kilometers (42.5 miles)
Estimated time: 1 day
Terrain: Very hilly
Map: Prince Edward Island Highway Map
Connecting tours: Tour Nos. 16 and 17
Connections: Trans-Canada Highways 1 and 2

This tour offers the island's most difficult, exciting, and challenging ride. The tour is steep; few flat sections exist. The route comprises four Heritage Roads with unpaved clay surfaces, each bordered by overhanging tree branches that provide shade and cozy protection. Don't let the protection fool you, however, as the roads can be rough due to heat bumps, rocks uncovered by frost, and stream runoff. The tour's history is limited; the explanations are basic. The tour feels as if you've entered and discovered another world where few other people have gone—mysterious even to most islanders. The route will challenge you physically, emotionally, and mentally. It will challenge your legs and endurance in the climbs, your heart and spirit over the clay roads, and your concentration and navigation through the turns and gullies. Be prepared with thick tires and sturdy equipment. There are no provisions available except at the beginning and end of the tour. Expect hot climbing. Wind is a non-factor because the trees act as windbreaks. You may find traveling on some of the clay roads impossible until late May due to lingering and melting snow.

Each component of this tour, from road conditions to food, is a factor to confront and triumph over. It's for serious fun. So enjoy a different PEI and a different aspect of adventure touring.

Victoria to Victoria: 70.2 kilometers

The tour starts at Victoria's lighthouse. Since the small town only has one main street, you should find the lighthouse easily. Start the tour by heading east over the causeway, keeping the wharf on your right. Follow the shore road, passing by well-manicured **Victoria Provincial Park**. Veer **left**, and 2.9 km from Victoria you're at the junction with **Trans-Canada Highway 1** at **Hampton**. A small convenience store sits about 50 meters down the highway to the left. Continuing up the hill, and after 1.3 km, the first stretch of red carpet welcomes you. Along these unpaved roads, remember that the inside curves are

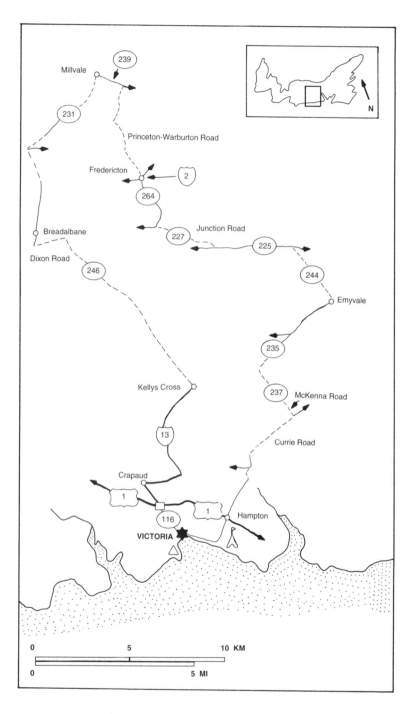

rougher than the outside due to water runoff that gouges the road. The red thread of road drops into the DeSable River Valley and will later follow its hilly shoulder. In 3.2 km from the Trans-Canada Highway you reach the junction for **246**. At the STOP sign turn **left**. In 600 meters take the first **right** onto unmarked **Currie Road**, the first of the Heritage Roads.

In 1987 the government decided it wanted to protect a part of the island's heritage—the old historic roads that once linked sections of the island. The first priority was to prevent the public and private landowners from altering the roads and bordering vegetation. From that point on, anyone who wanted to change the road or cut any bordering trees had to obtain written permission. The landowners entered into agreements to protect the strip of woodland or hedgerow next to the government's right-of-way. Now the trees, such as maples, oak, and spruce, arch over the road and provide nesting areas for song-birds and travel corridors for foxes, squirrels, and hares. Open areas beside the roads sprout wildflowers such as lupines, daisies, and trilli-ums. Where once wagon and horse traffic trundled across the island, farmers now use the cool shady paths to move between fields. Each twist and turn in the road is a small slice of adventure.

Currie Road, bordered by oak and hemlock trees, offers glimpses of the surrounding Bonshaw Hills and Northumberland Strait. The road was named for the Curries, early landowners. In the late 1800s and early 1900s horses and wagons hauled wood and meat to market along this road. Alone, you almost expect a settler on his wagon to amble past. Stay alert though, as parts of this road are sandy and can easily grab your wheel. You have a couple of steep sections to grunt over, but the road makes up for it with its views into the forest and fields of clover and daisies. The best view over the hills comes 3 km farther at the next intersection. At the STOP sign turn **left** onto **237**. You come to a fork after 2.5 km. Keep **right**. You're now on wooded **McKenna Road**, named after Hugh McKenna, another property owner. Before you reach the end of this road (I told you the hills would be steep) it becomes paved and opens up to a view over the farmers' quilted fields sewn together by tree-lined threads. You also get to see the next ridge of hills you have to climb over. At the end of **237**, after 2.8 km, turn **right** onto **235**. The signs point to North River. After 2.7 km, at **Emyvale**, turn **left** onto **244**. Ahead you can see the carpet of green hills rolling in front of you. Highway 244 becomes gravel as you come to a triangle of roads, but continue straight until the road ends; then turn **left** on **225** after a total of 3.4 km. Traffic can pick up slightly along this paved road, so be careful as you fly downhill and cross the intersection of 13 after 1.4 km. From the intersection 2.3 km, take the **second right** for **227**. If you've had enough of paved roads, here we go again. You enter **Junction Road**, passing by ninety-year-old hemlock trees and ditches filled with trillium and lady slippers. In the late 1800s sawmills operated at the road's northern end. After 3.6 km on the easiest of the Heritage Roads turn **right** at the STOP sign follow-ing paved **264**. In 3 km, at Fredericton, turn right onto Highway 2, which has more traffic along one 100-meter length than you'll see all

The author zips along unpaved Appin Road, one of the Heritage Roads.

day. After the third house on the left, 100 meters farther, turn **left** onto **Princeton-Warburton Road**. The road begins climbing over farmers' fields that provide a sense of seclusion and wilderness. The isolation can make you lose perspective on where you are; Cavendish is only 12 km away. **Princeton Road**, one of the most famous early roads, was once the main artery connecting Charlottetown to Princeton, the original capital of Prince County. The hilly road slips into a tunnel of trees as it winds into the Millvale Valley.

In another 5 km you arrive back on pavement. Turn **left** following the Millvale sign on **239**. The route slips beside the muddy-red Millvale River until you reach the village of **Millvale** with its working dam and small mill, 1.2 km farther. Turn **left** at the STOP sign on **231**. The next hill pounces on you, and at the top of the rolling ridge, stop and admire the grand views over the hills on either side of the road. Continue on 231 past 230 as the road alternates between gravel and pavement. Traveling along this winding road, after 7.6 km, you reach the junction for 2. Continue straight on **231**, and after 2.3 km you reach **Breadalbane**, which may have a convenience store. When I was there the decrepit general store, staffed by a hacking, chain-smoking man, only had dusty old items piled haphazardly on his paint-peeled shelves. Try not to depend on this stop for provisions. From Breadalbane, 500 meters farther turn **left** on **246**, **Dixon Road**. After 1.6 km, keep right at the forks. After another 4 km pass the junction for 225, and 300 meters farther you come to a Y **intersection**. Keep **left**, following the pavement, and after 200 meters keep **right** again. As you cycle along the next portion of paved ridge, have fun with the cows. Practice your "moo" and see how many cows give you the look that only cows can give. You may have thought you were done with unpaved roads, but you've one last roller-coasting section before you reach **Kelly's Cross**, 5.5 km from the last turn. Turn **left** onto **13** down to Crapaud. This stretch of highway provides a well-deserved downhill but also has a couple of hills to keep you honest. As you near Crapaud you can glimpse Victoria's harbor and lighthouse. Beyond Kelly's Corner 7 km you reach **Crapaud** and the junction with **Trans-Canada Highway 1**. Turn **left** on **1 East**. Enjoy the broad comfortable shoulder for 2.7 km until you veer **right** at the red-and-white steeple of the Presbyterian church, where you follow **116**. Soon, you re-enter the town of **Victoria**, known for its theater productions, but the biggest buildings are the still-used barns. Before you crash into the shore when the road ends after 2 km, turn **left** on the main street, and 200 meters farther you're back at the lighthouse.

TOUR NO. 16

THE DUNES TOUR

Start / Finish: Cavendish/Cavendish
Distance: 88.5 kilometers (44 miles)
Estimated time: 1 day
Terrain: Slightly rolling to hilly
Map: Prince Edward Island Highway Map
Connecting tours: Tour Nos. 15 and 18
Connections: Highways 13 and 15

The Dunes tour is an impressionist palette. Vivid colors blur, dance, and change in the shifting sunlight. The terracotta cliffs absorb the sunlight like clay moldings while the sea sparkles like an azure carpet littered with diamonds. Large cotton balls roll on a blue-sky easel, the sunlight dappling the fields with every imaginable hue of green. Farmers' houses, bright yellow, red, and blue, stand joyfully in fields of white-blossoming potato plants and beaming yellow sunflowers. Beside the houses, purple and pink lupines play in the wind. As the sun sets on the golden dunes, colors become more mute as shadows cradle the delicate hues of sand, sea, and sky.

Despite the tour's 88-km length, it could stretch easily to 2 or 3 days. Lazy days on beaches and flavorful sights can entice you into longer stays. Luckily, there are numerous bailouts where you can shorten the trip if one of the beaches has seduced you to lie around a little longer. Although the area around Cavendish is a crush of tawdry tourism, including heavy traffic, once you've maneuvered through it the rest of the tour is surprisingly quiet and easygoing.

The wind may be your most ferocious adversary or joyous ally, depending on your direction. Traveling west to east, the tour should take advantage of the offshore winds and, in the interior, the trees should offer a windbreak.

Supplies are sporadic. Your best bets are Cavendish, North and South Rustico, and Oyster Bed Bridge. Supplies are unavailable in the national park. The only bike shop is in Charlottetown, but there is bike rental available at Cavendish.

Cavendish to Cavendish: 88.5 kilometers

The tour begins at the junction of Highways 6 and 13. Before you start, visit the grave of Lucy Maud Montgomery, PEI's most famous author and, arguably, one of Canada's best-known writers. A small walkway

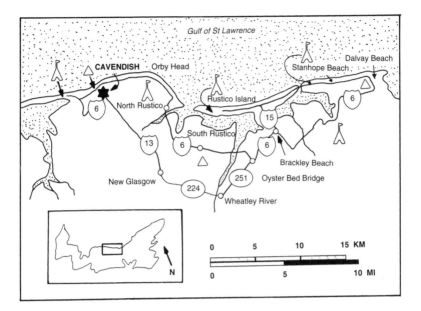

leads to a flower-encircled grave and tombstone. Past the intersection 100 meters is the **left** turn for **Green Gables**, the setting for Lucy Maud Montgomery's *Anne of Green Gables*.

Back on **6**, you now have to pass the Cavendish sideshow. Amusement parks, entertainment centers, oddities museum, and campgrounds that look like RV dealerships combine to make this stretch of road the worst on the island. Fortunately, you have to contend with it for only 2.3 km, then you turn **right** at the first righthand-turn lane, following the signs for Cavendish Beach and Prince Edward Island National Park. The placid road leads you to the park entrance 1.5 km farther (no need to stop if you are on your bike). To your left 200 meters is **Cavendish Campground**. If you want to take an interesting side trip, follow the signs for the Homestead Bike Trail, a crushed-gravel hiking and biking trail that follows the inner beach lagoon and then turns inland past sown fields and forgotten farm buildings.

Continuing to hop and skip on the park road, after 1.1 km you come to the **right** turn for the parking area at **Cavendish Beach**, one of the tour's best beaches. Follow a boardwalk to reach the sandy shore backed by 18-meter-high dunes. The boardwalk protects the precarious dune system from the invasion of tourists who might otherwise clomp through the area disrupting the fragile ecosystem.

The ecosystem begins with the sea. Waves pound into the headlands and cliffs to crush the rock into countless grains of sand. The local currents and strong winds carry the sand toward the shore, depositing it as sandbars and beach. The winds pick up the sand and carry it down the beach until a piece of driftwood or clump of grass slows down the

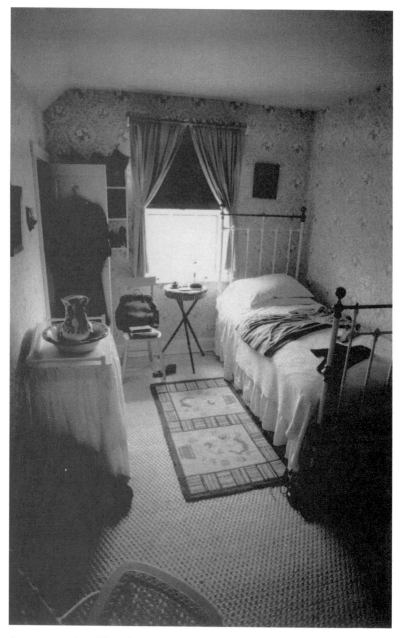

A reconstruction of how Anne of Green Gables' room at Green Gables may have looked at the turn of the century.

wind, causing the sand to drop and begin accumulating. A new dune is born. Marram grass begins to grow, acting as an anchor that attracts more sand to the dune. It grows higher. The sand-loving grass is the key to the system's survival. Its root system can stretch 3 meters into the dunes, tangling into an intense web and helping the dune to stay together. Marram grass is hardy; it can grow quickly to the surface after being buried by storms and its graceful curved blades help it to withstand the salt spray, but one human footstep can crush a clump of grass. Once a link of the anchor chain disintegrates, the wind carves small depressions into giant holes, called blowouts. Too many blowouts and any vegetation on the dunes begins to die.

Trace the line of towering dunes along the park road until you break free and follow the quiet, rolling terrain past stunning views of red cliffs dropping into the blue sea. About 5 km from Cavendish Beach you come to **Orby Head**, offering magnificent views up and down the northern coast of the island. **Cape Turner Picnic Area** (drinking water) lies another 1.2 km farther. Three km along you arrive at **Rustico Beach**, marked by the harbor and quiet beach. You leave the park, and 1.2 km farther along, you arrive in bustling **North Rustico**. There is no bridge to Rustico Island from this end so you must slip down beside Rustico Bay to reenter the park. North Rustico has full provisions, including lobster suppers and a supermarket. You can return to Cavendish if you turn right back along busy 6 West. But rolling along **6 East** straight ahead, after 4 km you come to another bail-out junction, 258, which combined with 13 will take you back to Cavendish. Keep left, following scenic 6 for about 2 km until you arrive at the resort area around **South Rustico**, named for an Acadian settler, René Rassicot, who arrived from Normandy in 1724. Acadians settled and still live in the area. The most important feature in town is Belcourt's Bank, once Canada's smallest chartered bank.

Leaving South Rustico on 6, after 5.5 km of slightly rolling hills turn **left**, staying on **6** at **Oyster Bed Bridge**. You can take 251 now if you're running short on time (the tour returns to this point), otherwise for the next 3.7 km the road dips into a small valley, coming to **15**. Turn **left**. For the next 3 km you pass the Dunes Studio Gallery (a stunning blend of art, architecture, and landscaping), the short road to the village of Brackley Beach, and the national park entrance. At the end of the busy road, you arrive at another of the park's popular beaches, Brackley. If you've had enough cycling for the day you can head to the primitive campground at Rustico Island. Ask at the park administration office about the availability of potable water at the secluded campground before you cycle the 4 km. The road follows the dune system as it passes along the Gulf of St. Lawrence. The dunes reach humbling heights through this section and the Parks Department has restricted most of them to protect the endangered piping plover. The park shelters nearly 2 percent of the world's population of this small, secretive shorebird. The park likes to use the example of the piping plover to exemplify how tourists and nature can share a national park. Now, if only the less-rare, inconsiderate tourist would

An old iron wheel rim sits in a tangle of brush along the Homestead Bike Trail in Prince Edward Island National Park.

respect the area and stay off the dunes and out of the restricted areas the shore bird's population wouldn't be dropping.

Once past the picture-perfect Stanhope Lighthouse, the road passes a mélange of cottages, marshes, beaches, and campgrounds. After 7 km you pass **Stanhope Beach** campground, and 1.4 km farther you come to the start of the **Farmlands** and **Babbling Brook trails**. Each trail takes about 45 minutes, but the Babbling Brook Trail is the more interesting. Both pass the Stanhope Cemetery, an old secluded resting place for early settlers and victims of the Yankee gale, a horrific storm a century ago off the coast that claimed hundreds of fishermen's lives.

Less than a km farther along the park road you come to the **Reed and Rushes Trail**, a 0.5-km trail leading to an inland marsh and pond. Another 800 meters and you pass **Dalvay-by-the-Sea**, a grand hotel built last century for the rich and fashionable elite from Canada and New England. Across from the hotel is **Dalvay Beach**, a less-crowded stretch of sand. Beyond the hotel 2 km, passing along the shores of Dalvay Lake, you leave the park for the last time. Take the first **right** onto **6**. The road begins following a corridor of trees and then weaves between forest and farmlands. Stay on **6** through its twists and turns for 11 km until you reach **6's junction** with **15**. Follow the merger of 15 and 6 for 2.5 km until **6** turns **left** back to **Oyster Bed Bridge**. Return the 3.7 km along this previous section of road, but this time at the intersection for 6 continue **straight** on **251**. The roads along this section can be rough. The sandstone base the road crews used as roadbed becomes saturated with water in the spring, creating a soupy mixture underneath. The road bumps and swells, breaking up the surface asphalt. The road also becomes more hilly as it offers an intimate view of the small farming communities nestled in the valleys. From the junction, after 4.6 km, continue **right** on **224** over the bridge at **Wheatley River**, but keep right taking **224**. Another 6.5 km take you to **New Glasgow**, a small town nestled into the river valley.

Immediately after the bridge in New Glasgow, turn **right** onto **13**. This road has a few rolling hills you have to gear up for, but after about 10 km you're back at **Cavendish**.

TOUR NO. 17

FORT AMHERST TOUR

Start / Finish: Strathgartney Provincial Park/
Strathgartney Provincial Park
Distance: 66.6 kilometers (40.6 miles)
Estimated time: 1 day
Terrain: Hilly
Map: Prince Edward Island Highway Map
Connecting tours: Tour Nos. 15 and 16
Connections: Trans-Canada Highway 1

Most of this tour comprises a quiet ride along the Northumberland
Strait and over rolling farmland once inhabited by Micmacs and
Acadians. Today, the only historical evidence of their habitation is the
earthwork trenches of Port la Joye and Indian Village, the trip's
manmade sights. The ride slices along farmlands, kneads the rolling
hills, and slips between soupy marshes. The tour offers a great day trip
within sight of Charlottetown yet it's secluded enough to give you
quiet, idyllic riding. The weather is usually pleasant with winds generally from the southwest. The tour's only sore spot is the brief section of
the Trans-Canada Highway, but the road's wide, safe shoulder lessens
the traffic's effects.

Stock up on food before beginning this tour, as it's difficult to obtain.

Strathgartney Provincial Park to Strathgartney Provincial Park: 66.6 kilometers

The tour starts at **Strathgartney Provincial Park**, overlooking the
Bonshaw Hills and Northumberland Strait. If you're not camping here,
you may be interested in the park's summer interpretive programs and
hiking trails through the hills. From the **Trans-Canada Highway**, you
start downhill, away from Charlottetown. When you finish the initial descent, you pass the village of **Bonshaw**. After about 7.5 km of rolling
road, turn **left** onto placid **Highway 19**, part of the Blue Heron Drive.
After about 4 km of riding within sight of the Northumberland Strait
you pass **Argyle Shore Provincial Park**. This park boasts a quiet
beach, picnic facilities, and free hot showers. The road from Argyle
gently and quietly rolls beside the shore. Fragrances float in the air: the
sharp smell of pine, the nostalgic smell of hay, the ripe smell of cattle
barns, and the perfumed smell of wildflowers. Past the park 8 km, stay
right on 19 at **Canoe Cove**. Along this section of road you can see Nova
Scotia's sizable hills across the strait. As the road veers northward past

A couple dressed in Victorian costume takes a break from playing croquet to pose in front of the government house in Charlottetown.

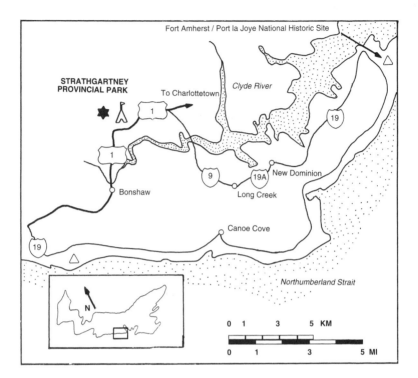

Rice Point, marking the entrance to Hillsborough Bay, you come to another fork 8 km farther. Keep **right** again. The road climbs slightly and follows a ridge. After about 8 more km, you come to the entrance to **Fort Amherst/Port la Joye National Historic Park**. To visit the site, cycle 400 meters to your **right**, viewing Charlottetown across the harbor.

Back on **19** continue downhill, being careful at the sharp left corner at the bottom. About 1.5 km from the park entrance is the Indian Village Craft Shop, which displays life-size replicas of a typical Micmac village. Keep on **19** to **New Dominion**, rolling past marsh, forest, and farmland. At the crossroads of town, 7 km from Indian Village, turn **left** onto **19A**. Follow this rolling road for about 5 km, dipping into **Long Creek** and MacLeods Creek until you reach the junction for **9**. Turn **right** on **9** and about 3 km farther—dropping into and over Clyde River—you climb back to the **Trans-Canada Highway**. Turn **left** and begin the trek back to the park. The Trans-Canada Highway, a fine road, dares you with one major climb before you return to **Strathgartney**, 4 km from the previous junction.

TOUR NO. 18

EAST POINT

Start / Finish: Red Point Provincial Park/Red Point
Provincial Park
Distance: 66.3 kilometers (40.4 miles)
Estimated time: 1 day
Terrain: Level to slightly rolling
Map: Prince Edward Island Highway Map
Connecting tours: Tour No. 19
Connections: Highways 2 and 4

This eclectic day tour through forests, seascapes, and pasture will appeal to each of your senses. Traveling down a cinnamon-colored Heritage Road, the canopy of verdant green trees creates a cool ambiance dappled by sunlight. On the north shore you can smell the tangy salt-water spray as the waves hush over the beaches like a primeval lullaby. From the Cyclopean lighthouse at East Point, the road jour-neys between fertile green potato fields tinged with white bursts of blossoms and, in the ditches, the pastel purples and pinks of lupines stretching to the sun and swaying in the sea-tinged breezes. Winds are changeable through the area as the cold, northern Labrador sea cur-rents from the northeast meet the warm, southern Gulf sea currents at East Point. This quiet tour will seduce you with its earth, sea, and sky.

You can find supplies at Souris and North Lake. Again, the island's only bike shop is in Charlottetown.

Red Point Provincial Park to Red Point Provincial Park: 66.3 kilometers

The tour starts at this provincial park 11 km east of Souris. You can leave a car here for a day. **Highway 16** begins rolling west past farms, cottages, and lupine-filled ditches. Quickly, the road swerves slightly inland past **Black Pond Bird Sanctuary**, and after nearly 11 km you enter **Souris**. Since the locals use the town as a supply depot, so should you. It's the most reliable town for provisions.

Pronounced *surrey,* the town was named by French settlers for the mice that the fishing crews inadvertently brought over. The rodents pro-liferated rapidly and quickly overran the town. In the early 1700s, the port, nestled on a quiet, sandy cove, was used as a base for seasonal European fishermen. Today, the wharf is still one of PEI's busiest ports, particularly during lobster season, when you can buy freshly caught

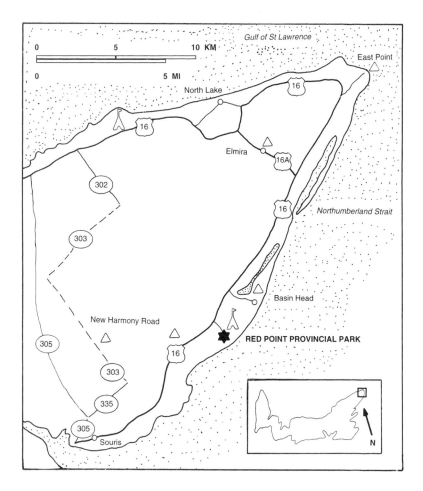

lobster straight off the boats. Just a couple of km from Souris is the ferry for the Magdalen Islands.

After passing through town, turn **right** on **Chapel Street (305)**. About 600 meters along you pass the deceptively solid-looking St. Mary's Church. The church was rebuilt twice after devastating fires, the last time in 1930, but even now the winds and rains are corroding the soft local sandstone. Past the church 700 meters turn **right** onto **335**. If you want to avoid the unpaved Heritage Road that follows, continue straight on 305 and then turn **right** on **16** toward East Point. After about 3 km, 335 ends and you turn **left** onto unpaved **303**. A little more than 1 km past the Heritage Road section of 303, **New Harmony Road** begins. The road passes through land that was once cleared and farmed by French, English, and Irish settlers, and later,

Skeletal Hawthorne bushes grow near the lighthouse at East Point.

during Prohibition, rum runners used the remote location to hide their unloaded contraband.

After entering the narrow tunnel of trees in about another km, you come to the right junction to the **New Harmony Demonstration Woodlot**. Managed by the PEI and Canadian governments, the 107 hectares of woodland were designed to show woodlot owners proper forest management and to teach visitors about the island's scarce forests. The woodlot has a 1-km trail, and with the brochure available on site or at the tourist office in Souris (300 meters west of Chapel Avenue) you can learn about forestry management. Just bring plenty of insect repellent.

Back on **303**, after 1.3 km, the Heritage Road section ends, the road widens, and you pass the junction with 304. Continue straight along this level, usually well-maintained part of 303. There may be sections however, where woodcutters, dragging their equipment along the road, have chewed up some spots. From the junction 2.2 km, keep **right** at the Y intersection, staying on **303**. About 6 km farther on 303, turn **left** onto paved **302** (**Baltic Road**). Four km later 302 ends, and you turn **right** onto **16** (**North Shore Road**). Rolling through woodlands and trails another 4 km, you pass **Campbells Cove Provincial Park**. Another 4 km take you to the junction to **North Lake**. You can either turn left and go through PEI's blue-fin tuna capital, or continue straight and climb the ridge that offers a gorgeous view of the town, harbor, and seascape. Both routes join again shortly. Just 2 km from the junction along 16 you come to 16A, which heads to Elmira and the train museum. Depending on your timing (the museum is open from 9:00 A.M. to 5:00 P.M.), you can visit the museum at this junction or after East Point.

The museum lies about 1.5 km from Highway 16. The one-story building has been restored as a replica of the eastern terminus for PEI's railway. The small museum displays memorabilia and photographs that interpret the railway's history.

Back on **16**, the road slips closer to the coast, over a low-lying marsh, and after 7.5 km you come to the turn for **East Point Lighthouse**. Another 2 km east and you arrive at the island's most eastern tip. The Micmac knew the area as *kespemenagek*, meaning "the end of the island." Here, the two tides from the Northumberland Strait and the Gulf of St. Lawrence surge together in front of the lighthouse. Today, the lighthouse is the only one of three on the island still staffed. You can take a guided tour of the privately owned and operated, 186-meter-high wooden structure and listen to some of the stories the guide narrates.

As you return to Highway 16 you can see Cape Breton Highlands across the strait. At night the lighthouses from Nova Scotia wink across the water at Prince Edward Island. Another 5 km past the turn for East Point you pass the last junction for 16A to Elmira. Continue straight as the road begins rolling through fields of lupines, red and blue barns, and deserted, gray-weathered farm buildings. The road for Basin Head lies 7 km down the road. Basin Head, 1.5 km to the left on

Visitors walk along the shore at East Point, where the two tides of Prince Edward Island meet.

a side road, holds two notable features: the Fisheries Museum and the "singing sands."

The museum, a small complex of buildings, offers insight into the history of the region's commercial fishing by displaying original equipment, dioramas, and photographs. Below the main building stand fish shacks and a replica of an old lobster cannery. Closer to the sea is Basin Head's second most noteworthy sight, the "singing sands." Because of the high silica content of the beach's sand, when you walk on it the sand emits a high-pitched squeak. Regardless of whether you think it sounds like singing or screeching, the beaches along this section are some of the finest white beaches on the island. Return to **Red Point Provincial Park** after 2 km, where you can relax on the beach.

TOUR NO. 19

DOWN EAST

Start/Finish: Pooles Corner (Montague)/Montague
Distance: 133.8 kilometers (81.5 miles)
Estimated time: 2 days or 1 long one
Terrain: Flat to slightly rolling
Map: Prince Edward Island Highway Map
Connections: Highways 1 and 4; Wood Islands Ferry to Nova Scotia

Islanders use the term "Down East" with a certain derision. People from the island's center make jokes and feel that people from Down East are hicks and hillbillies. However, along your travels through a rolling rural landscape speckled with harbors and lighthouses you'll find some of the friendliest people on PEI, from the captain of Cap'n Murph's Seal Tours to the guides of Orwell Historic Village. Most travelers disembark from the Woods Island Ferry and dash along the Trans-Canada Highway to Charlottetown, ignoring the charm the area has to offer. Be aware, however, that finding supplies between Murray Harbour and Montague is difficult and the winds can be gusty, blowing from the southwest. This Down East tour is an idyllic ride of pastoral landscapes, natural history, and hospitality.

Pooles Corner to Northumberland Provincial Park: 81.2 kilometers

The tour begins at the junction for **Highways 4** and **3** across from the **Kings Byway Visitor's Centre**. The center houses a comprehensive introduction to the region, displaying the history, economy, and architecture of the area. Brudnell River Provincial Park, offering camping and bike trails, lies a few kilometers to the east along Highway 3. Start this tour by heading south along **Highway 4**, and immediately you are confronted with a short stepped hill up to **Montague**. The next 4.5 km to **Main Street** in town has a paved shoulder, so although the traffic is fairly busy for PEI standards you can stay well off to the side. The traffic in town is a little messier but easily tolerable.

British settlers established the foundations that would become the port and commercial center for logging and shipping on the southeastern end of the island. To learn about the development of Montague and the region, stop at the **Garden of the Gulf Museum**, just after the bridge at the center of town. The former post office, overlooking the Montague River, is worth stopping at to view the farm implements, textile collection, and 1698 Bible.

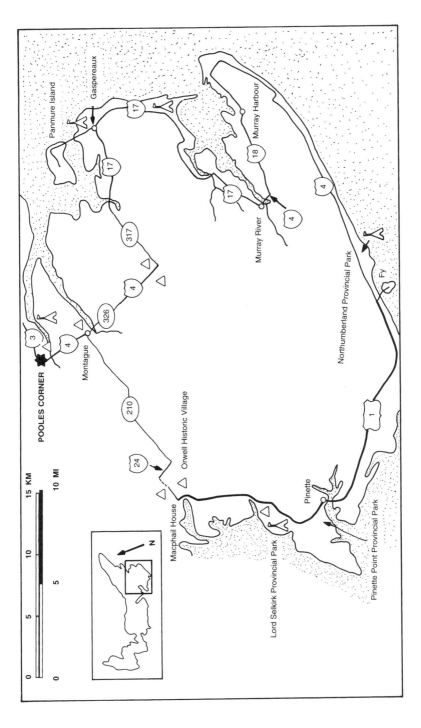

As you leave town you face a steep climb, and 1.1 km from the museum turn **right** following **326**. This short road ends in a km when you turn **left** at the STOP sign on **Highway 4**. The road begins rolling gently past forest and farmland for a little over 5 km to the **Harvey Moore Wildlife Management Area**.

A km from the wildlife management area take the **left** on 317 and arrive almost instantly at **Buffaloland Provincial Park**. This frivolous attraction attempts to display the buffalo and deer in their habitat. A long fenced path takes you to the middle of a field where you can try to spot the animals. Sometimes they can be right below you, and other times they can be resting in the forest.

Back onto **317** the road rolls past woodlands and streams dotted with abandoned farm buildings. In about 6 km you turn **right** onto hilly **17 South**. Almost 7 km farther, after passing the almost fictional town of **Gasperaux**, is the turn left on 347 for **Panmure Island Provincial Park**. This beautiful little park offers camping and one of the island's best white-sand beaches.

The next section of road, blipping and dipping along, offers views over Nova Scotia's Antigonish highlands and Georges Bay until you reach the junction for Seal Cove Campground after 9 km. Turn **left**, continuing on **17** after 800 meters. You cycle along flat road that follows the Murray River and its tributary streams and inlets. Through the chinks in the forest you can spot small wharves and co-op mussel harvesting farms on the harbor banks. Highway 17 ends after 8.5 km, and you turn **left** on **4 South**. After 800 meters take the **left** at the STOP sign, continuing on **4**, which cuts through the town of **Murray River** a short 400 meters farther.

Murray River is a jaunty little town offering craft shops and seal-watching cruises. The tour also incorporates a swing past the mussel harvesting areas and Bird Island, where cormorants and gulls nest in the denuded tree stalks.

A km from the town's wharf turn **left** on **18**, and after 6.5 km you come to **Murray Harbour**, your last reliable chance for provisions to get you to Montague. The engaging town of Murray Harbour has a history of fishing. The Micmac called the area Eskwaser, meaning "fishing place." To the present fleet of thirty-five fishing boats, fishing is the town's lifeblood. Mussels, oysters, lobster, and tuna are all canned at the processing plants along the harbor. In 0.5 km from the wharf, turn **left** onto **18**. A km to the right is the Log Cabin Museum, a small house displaying antiques and a doll collection. Highway 18 has a few small hills, and in about 5.5 km the road bends to the right. On the other side of the trees you hear the pulse of the waves as they hit the shore, but you don't see them for another 1.5 km until the trees disappear. Any wind hits you head on, and you can only admire the impressive views over the Northumberland Strait to Nova Scotia. Continue on 18 until it ends, changes to **4**, and carries through beside the strait. After 21.3 km of rolling landscape past potato farms and pastureland you arrive at **Northumberland Provincial Park** with its 1-km-long red sand beach.

Northumberland Provincial Park to Montague: 52.6 kilometers

From the park, continue along **Highway 4**, and after 2.5 km pass the junction for Wood Islands Ferry. The highway shifts into **Trans-Canada Highway 1** as the road carries along over slightly wrinkled terrain. Traffic moves to the rhythm of the ferry, and you can make a game out of spotting the various license plates that pass you when the ferry passengers disembark. The road rolls along for 18 km past farmlands festooned with giant marshmallow-shaped hay bales until you reach **Pinette Point Provincial Park**, a small day park overlooking a cute harbor silhouetted against the red-serrated cliffs. The road becomes more hilly after **Pinette**, and shortly afterward you pass the junction to 209, heading 11 km to Point Prim, which holds the oldest lighthouse on PEI. About 4.5 km from Pinette you pass **Lord Selkirk Provincial Park**, and almost immediately after you pass the **British Royalty Collection**. This array of over 200 items of Royal Family memorabilia looks as though it has been tucked into someone's garage. The road continues through hilly but relaxed terrain. After about 8.5 km, you reach the junction to **210**. If you are worried about the small section of dirt between Orwell and Highway 24, return along this road

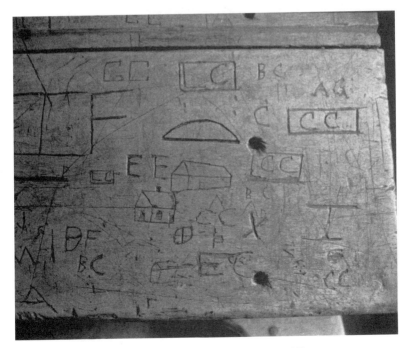

A desktop at the school house at Orwell Corner Historic Village

At the lumberjack show in Montague, a participant readies himself to row a barrel across the harbor.

after visiting **Orwell Historic Village** only 600 meters farther to the **right**.

Orwell Historic Village is Atlantic Canada's smallest re-created village. Comprising eight buildings, from blacksmith's shop to community hall, the village attempts to re-create a rural village of the late nineteenth century. Costumed guides and interpreters raise small crops and livestock as they go about the chores of this village crossroads. The site has activities throughout the summer, including festivals, craft lessons, and demonstrations.

Upon returning to the village road, instead of retracing your pedaling to **210** turn **right** toward **Macphail House** 1.3 km farther, partly on a clay road.

Sir Andrew Macphail was one of Prince Edward Island's most famous sons; there were few fields that did not interest him, and he provided a model for intellectuals of the period. A physician, an author, and the first professor of medical history at McGill University, he was born at this house and went to school in a small schoolhouse at Uigg, a few kilometers from here. This renaissance man was also founder of *The Canadian Medical Association Journal*, and at the age of fifty he enlisted with the ambulance corps, serving the front-line troops for twenty months. Upon his return he spent his summers with his family at this house, developing new strains of potato plants and writing *The Master's Wife*, a story of local Scottish immigrants.

From the parking lot turn **left** back onto the dirt road, a km farther turn **right** onto **24**, and a little less than 2 km later turn **left** onto **210**. This portion of the tour feels the most remote as the road passes large-acreage farms planted with potatoes, grain, and tobacco. A few farm-houses and tobacco drying sheds break up the expansive landscape as the road rolls along with gusto. Along 210 11 km, you arrive back at **Montague's Main Street**. The Garden Gulf Museum is about 600 meters to your right and the **Visitor's Centre**, the original starting point, is about 5 km to your **left**.

NEWFOUNDLAND

INTRODUCTION

Geography

The total area of the island of Newfoundland and mainland Labrador is almost 300,000 square kilometers. The island itself is only 70,000 square kilometers of that. Since the cycling opportunities are limited to Newfoundland, I don't include Labrador in this book.

Newfoundland looks like a complex piece of a giant jigsaw puzzle. Jagged peninsulas reach into the sea. The relentless waves carve deep harbors into the land. The island's austere terrain slopes gradually from west to east. Although the rocky outcroppings and treeless horizons seem ageless, before the Europeans arrived forest covered the low-lying parts of the island. Relentless European exploitation denuded and burnt the land into sterilization. Once you reach the natural barrens above 100 meters, the wind and weakened soil produce a stark landscape.

Hundreds of gannets circle above a fishing trawler at Cape St. Mary's.

On the barrens and through the isolated wilds of Newfoundland a wide range of animals roam and thrive. On the southern peninsulas, caribou, in herds of thousands, graze and migrate. Moose, introduced on the island this century, dunk in the sloughs. Beaver, rabbits, and foxes scuttle, hop, and weave along the land.

Newfoundland is also home to some of the largest bird colonies in North America. Cape St. Mary's provides a nesting area for 60,000 gannets; Witless Bay Ecological Reserve protects tens of thousands of puffins. Out to sea, sprightly seals and majestic whales follow the smelt migration that flourishes where the cold Labrador Current and the warm Gulf Stream meet. If you want an opportunity to see a multitude of wildlife, untainted by overvisitation, visit the wilds of Newfoundland.

The people of Newfoundland, particularly those in the outports (everything outside St. John's, the capital), maintain a simple life based on natural resources. They've always been the butt of Canadian jokes. When the storyteller needs the simpleton or blunderhead, it is always a "Newfie." Yet, these "Newfies" are probably the most friendly, warm-hearted people in Canada. The years of isolation have provided Canada with a colorful group of people. Yet a cloud of despair hangs over the islanders' heads. Cod was the island's currency; from the delicacy of cod tongue to cod liver oil to daily cod jiggin', their identity and lives depended on the fish. The Grand Banks, a long shelf of land beneath the sea where the ocean currents meet, had provided prosperity. John Cabot, in 1497, wrote of being able to lower a basket into the water and raise it filled with fish. But for a multitude of reasons, the fishery has been decimated. Fingers of blame point in every direction: foreign overfishing, government mismanagement, illegal inshore fishermen, and the cessation of the seal hunt. The combination of reasons has caused the government to institute a cod moratorium. No one is allowed to fish, and the Royal Canadian Navy now patrols the waters, even outside its 200-mile jurisdiction. The present-day scenario leaves the fishery moribund. Most people say it will never come back; the optimists say that they see large schools of cod and it won't be long until they are back in their boats jiggin'. Sadly, the traditional Newfoundland culture is disappearing and the islanders struggle. It may not be until the next generation, growing up without a "fishocracy," that a new identity will emerge.

History

For thousands of years, aboriginal people have wandered through the forests and paddled along the shores of the island. The initial groups, the Maritime Archaic Indians and the Paleo-Eskimos, settled around Bonavista Bay and Port au Choix. What happened to these two groups is unknown, but archaeologists speculate climatic and ecological changes forced them to migrate south. The origin of the Beothuk Indians, the indigenous group that lived on the island when the Europeans arrived and is now extinct, is unknown as well.

Many of us were taught in school that Columbus discovered the New

World. Then we learned that Norsemen, exiled from Scandinavia, roamed the North Atlantic and settled in Iceland, Greenland, and Newfoundland. Yet how many of us know the accounts of the Irish voyage in 580 A.D., 500 years earlier than the Vikings? The writings of *The Voyage of Saint Brendan* detail an account of the wanderings of Abbot Brendan. His entourage of fourteen monks sailed the North Atlantic, ran into absurd adventures, and visited lands that were too fantastic to believe. Yet like Homer's *Odyssey* the writings may hold clues that the Irish were the first Europeans to land in the *New Founde Land*. In 1976, Tim Severin made the voyage under the same conditions as St. Brendan. His crew built and loaded ox-hide boats, and after spending 110 days at sea, journeying from Ireland to Iceland to Newfoundland, they found some of the same landmarks St. Brendan poetically described; the demon who hurled fire was the volcano on Iceland, and the "floating crystal columns" were icebergs flowing south from the polar ice cap. Although historians still disagree about the first European visitation, the possibility of Irish voyages is intriguing.

A majestic schooner glides past the lighthouse that signals the entrance to St. John's harbor.

St. Brendan may not have reached Newfoundland, but historians definitively know that Vikings sailed the North Atlantic. Despite historians' beliefs that the Norse sagas were only myths, the proof of Viking settlement was indisputable when an archaeologist uncovered the remains of a Viking settlement at L'Anse aux Meadows. The only controversy remaining is whether the site is Leif Erikson's Vinland. Was it the land of wild wheat, grapes, and wilderness utopia? No one can definitively answer that question yet, but we do know that the Vikings reached the New World 350 years before Columbus.

Newfoundland waters attracted European seafarers for generations. The waters, rich in whale and cod, brought the French, Basque, and Portuguese. The first recorded voyage to Newfoundland was that of John Cabot in 1497. His claim laid the foundation of England's Atlantic stronghold. England claimed the land, and every nation exploited the fishing grounds.

In 1610 John Guy started a private enterprise in the Cupid/Conception Bay area. The company gave Guy's colonists enough food for twelve months, along with tools, implements, artisans, and orders. In the first year, the colony built homes and workhouses, cleared land, and sowed grain. The first two winters were abnormally mild, and the colony was buoyant with success. The third winter treated the settlers harshly. Eight of the sixty-six colonists succumbed to scurvy and beriberi. The livestock died due to a lack of fodder. The following April, Guy returned to England, dealing a psychological and administrative blow to the colony. Only thirty colonists remained, and capital for the company became a problem. Compared to England's other colonies, such as Virginia, Newfoundland never received enough investment. Pirates frequently plundered the colony, and political pressure from the fishers eventually caused Newfoundland's first colony to fizzle.

Weather always played a role in colonization. Lord Baltimore tried to establish Ferryland in 1621 but stayed only one harsh winter until he left for New England. Slowly, the English presence continued to grow. By 1650, 500 residents lived in 40 colonies between Cape Bonavista and Trepassey. Thirty years later there were 2,000 English-speaking residents, including those brought by Guy, Baltimore, and the "bye-boatmen," seasonal fishers, from England.

The French controlled the island's south shore. A significant war started in 1689, and its turning point came when in 1696 France ravaged 36 English settlements and killed 200 people. The English retaliated and recaptured the settlements, securing their position in Newfoundland. Through various treaties, England gained control of the entire island, and to compensate for losing its fishing bases in Newfoundland France was granted St. Pierre and Miquelon to use as a shelter for French fishing crews. Today, the French fishing zone is still debated and quarreled over.

Up to the 1700s Newfoundland was governed by an admiralty system. Whatever captain arrived at the port became the "fishing admiral," responsible to maintain law and order in the harbor. But this ad hoc basis continued to be a source of trouble for the colonists since most captains didn't stay all year. Conditions degenerated, and the Beothuk were casualties.

The Beothuk avoided Europeans. As the fishing crews took over the harbors and beaches, the Beothuk withdrew into the forest and lost their seaside summer encampments. The colonists' expansion and influence increased. They became seal hunters in spring, salmon fishers in the summer, and trappers in the winter. The Beothuk, continually pushed into more isolated areas, faced starvation and could no longer rely on their traditional sources of food and clothing. Whenever the two groups met, violence erupted. Settlers chased them and raided their camps, and the Beothuk retaliated, killing a dozen settlers. The settlers avenged the revenge and killed the Beothuk indiscriminately. In 1823, three starving Beothuk women surrendered to a British settler. The mother and one daughter died of tuberculosis shortly afterward, but Shanadithit, the second daughter who Europeans called Nancy, lived for six years. During that time, she lived with a justice of the peace, relating information about her people. On June 16, 1829, the last of the Beothuk died.

In 1855, Newfoundland achieved self-government. The settlements continued to expand, and the island remained independent. Many islanders were suspicious of confederation with Canada. Their long-held animosity with the French, who comprised a third of Canada's population, was one cause of apprehension. Also, one-third of the islanders were Irish whose parents and grandparents had been persecuted by the English. After the Second World War, the New-foundland economy rebounded, and the government held a referendum on joining Canada. Canada, now realizing the island's strategic importance in the North Atlantic, encouraged Newfoundland's confederation. By only a 2-percent margin, Newfoundlanders in 1949 decided to become Canada's newest province.

We can't leave Newfoundland history without mentioning Premier Joey Smallwood. Newfoundland's "George Washington" dragged Newfoundland into the twentieth century. He diversified the economy, offered large incentives to large foreign corporations, and reformed education. In 1949 two-thirds of Newfoundland schools had only one room and lacked electricity. The government built new schools, trained teachers, and transformed Memorial College into a university.

Since Smallwood left politics in 1972, the usual depressed economy has sunk lower. The island's main employer, the fishing industry, has shut down and the unemployment rate nears 30 percent. Private consultants believe that for Newfoundland to be economically viable half the population will have to leave. A mood of despair hangs over the province as it looks for a new path into the future.

Weather

Ocean currents play the lead role in Newfoundland weather. From the north, the Labrador current, feeding from the polar ice, sweeps the northern coast. Icebergs commonly drift within sight of the island. This

A cyclist passes a sign warning of caribou crossings.

cold current tempers the summer climate. Rarely will a heat wave grip the island, and average summer temperatures are about 16 degrees Celsius. The Gulf Stream, fed by the warm waters of the Gulf of Mexico, flows past the southern Avalon Peninsula. The meeting of the currents produces some of the thickest, most lingering fog on the east coast. The fog can last for days, although a few kilometers inland the weather can be bright and sunny. Only when a new front adjusts the temperature or a strong wind blows the fog away can you appreciate the beauty of the land.

The winds in Newfoundland can be distressing for a cyclist. The shifting currents and the changeable weather produce winds of epic proportions, from Gros Morne where wind speeds can reach 90 kilometers per hour to the more docile, yet frustrating, winds around the Avalon Peninsula. In early spring the winds arrive from the east. It was this wind pattern that Basque whalers and French fishing crews explored as they worked the waters around the island. As the spring progresses, the wind shifts clockwise to the southwest and west. By late summer the prevailing winds are usually from the west. Don't count on a pattern, however. Winds shift crazily and storms can whip in from the clashing weather fronts. Just remember the advice of the islanders, some of whose lives depend on forecasting the weather: When gulls fly high, stormy weather can be expected. When distant hills appear near, rainy weather is coming. When the wind is in the east 'tis neither good for man nor beast. And, mackerel sky and mares' tails make the sailor furl his sails.

Accommodations

Distances in Newfoundland are larger than in other parts of the Maritimes. Isolated pockets of population make finding formal accommodations difficult. Even in the most populated section, the Avalon Peninsula, finding any type of accommodations can be a challenge, although this is more true in the south than in the north. Plan your accommodations arrangements carefully and bring a shelter for emergencies or drastic weather changes.

Tents are useful in Newfoundland. National and provincial parks offer camping areas, but they are usually spaced too far apart for bicycle tourists to use consistently. Private campgrounds are sometimes no more than an empty field with a portable toilet. Even some of the provincial parks' campgrounds lack wet toilets and showers. The people of Newfoundland readily accept free-camping and have raised it to an art form themselves—"pit-campers" they're called. In summer, vacationers will haul their trailers and campers to the abandoned pits once used in building the Trans-Canada Highway. Campers then set up in the pits. A row of them becomes a small community. Cycling past, you can smell the salmon cooking over the barrel-drum fires. If you are going to be in the outdoors, Newfoundlanders will expect you to camp, and if you ask permission you'll rarely be refused.

TOUR NO. 20

SOUTHERN AVALON

Start / Finish: Argentia/Argentia
Distance: 488.1 kilometers (298 miles)
Estimated time: 7 days
Terrain: Rugged
Maps: Southern Avalon Touring Route;
Newfoundland and Labrador Official
Highway Map
Connecting tours: Tour No. 21
Connections: Trans-Canada Highway; ferry
between Argentia and Sydney, Nova
Scotia

Avalon seems molded by the hand of God. The ferry from Sydney glides into the harbor as the shimmers of daylight cast a blue glow over the landscape. Rock monoliths rise out of the water like fingers from a desperately grasping hand. In the bay, whales, in their never-ending search for caplin, leave their footprints of still water on the ocean's surface. Avalon humbles as you look upon immortality.

This long, varied tour offers the bike traveler hard, rewarding cycling. Roads dip into settlements snuggled against the harbor, only to climb another hundred meters and cross lonely barrens. Radio towers, signaling the top of the climb, become your friends as you reach the barren heights, haunted by the wisps of fog that scoot across the landscape like wraiths. Then you descend into the next harbor to begin the cycle again. In secret corners you find small treasures: a pink sandstone beach, an ancient French fort, and a web-like waterfall. Southern Avalon teems with wildlife. On the barrens, herds of caribou, numbering up to 6,000 per herd, stop traffic for hours. Moose amble through bogs. At Cape St. Mary's 100,000 gannets and murres nest on a massive sea stack, and all that separates you from it is a 5-meter chasm. In the rolling ocean, whales chase the caplin migration, and in the translucent rivers salmon headed upstream frantically jump out of the water to inch forward to their spawning streams.

You have to rely on your ingenuity on this tour. Provisions are difficult to find; some lonely sections stretch up to 60 km before you can stock up with food and water. The tour's only bike shop is in St. John's. The almost 130-km section from Branch to Gaskiers Bay offers no formal accommodations. You'll have to rely on free-camping or ask for permission at villages along the route. The busiest section is the Trans-Canada Highway, which is being widened on a continual basis. Traffic between Ferryland and St. John's can be busy on weekends.

Most islanders are friendly and eager to help. Although at times self-absorbed with their current problems, the area's hardened villagers have relied on kinship and community values. You'll always be greeted with a "great day," even if it's pouring down rain. Unfortunately,

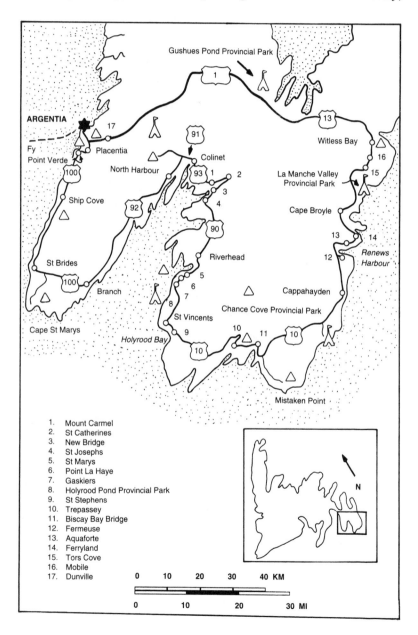

Atop Signal Hill stands the tower commemorating St. John's bicentennial in 1896.

mauzy (mist, drizzle, and fog) weather can be common on the south shore. Winds predominate from the west and southwest. Be prepared for total self-sufficiency and remember the Newfoundland saying, "An old dog for a hard road."

Argentia to St. Bride's: 55.1 kilometers

The ferry building is a free-for-all. Passengers, waiting or disembarking from the ferry, sleep and shower within the terminal. The current schedule has the Sydney ferry arriving in Argentia at dusk—not much time to get anywhere. Luckily, you can camp safely on the building grounds or stay inside, stretched out on the seats. Sleeping at the terminal is a common practice and everyone accepts it.

As you leave the terminal, head toward the toll booths and the road to Placentia. If you had to stay overnight at the terminal, the road will be deserted—the traffic is long gone. After about 3.5 km, traversing the deserted United States naval base, you reach the top of the first hill and the **Tourist Information Centre**. Pick up maps and other information here. In another 300 meters, turn **right** on **100**. After less than a kilometer, you pass the intersection for Freshwater, and 600 meters farther you come to a road to the **right** for **Castle Hill National Historic Park**. A side road reaches up the hill to the Visitor Information Centre, 900 meters off 100.

Castle Hill offers a realistic portrayal of the lives of the first settlers of Placentia. In the early 1500s Basques would sail over in the spring and stay until late summer, fishing for cod and fighting with the French over who controlled the ideal beach for drying fish and the bountiful fishing grounds. (The Canadian government is still battling foreigners over the rights to fishing on the Grand Banks.) The French first founded "Plaisance" in 1662 as a counterbalance against British expansion in Newfoundland.

Today, you can walk among the ruins and wooded slopes admiring the strategic position the fort had over the harbor. It's easy to imagine the importance of this point of land.

Back on **100**, only 2 km farther, you come to the town of **Placentia**. This friendly town offers full provisions, so stock up here for the ride to St. Bride's. The townspeople are used to travelers; storekeepers will ask where you're going, where you're from, and discuss the local goings-on.

The road skips through town, and 2.8 km later, squeezing between Southeast Arm Point and Point Verde Hill, you turn right, staying on **100**. (If you want to skip the most barren, most difficult, and most beautiful part of the tour, stay on partially unpaved 91, arriving in Colinet 38 km away.) From the junction, **100** climbs slightly, passing scattered houses and shacks that comprise the community of **Point Verde**. The stark barrenness begins to overwhelm you. The treeless landscape is reduced to shore, sea, and sky. Skeletal trees haunt the coast. Black rocks defy the pounding surf. The lonely screeches of gulls carry across the briny winds. On the barrens, the spirit-like fog sweeps across your path. In front of you, the road rolls, plummeting to the shoreline, and then relentlessly scales the next hill. This stretch of coastline is the most mesmerizing but is also the most difficult part of the tour. The road offers one staggering view after another, but the day's toughest hill is out of **Ship Cove**, where you have a 130-meter climb. On the other side of this barren is **Gooseberry Cove Provincial Park**, 25 km from the junction with 91. Red and purple rocks flank the beach tucked between the cliffs. From the park, the road continues to undulate. You might be able to get provisions along the way at the small unreliable home-convenience stores, but **St. Bride's** is the most reliable. Inhabited by descendants of the original Irish settlers, this isolated community lies 20 km farther from Gooseberry Cove. This small port is trying to benefit from the recent developments at Cape St. Mary's, and a tourist resort has opened.

St. Bride's to Colinet: 100.1 kilometers

Continue through town until the road veers sharply to the **left** where you find the town's main food store. From here, the road climbs gently for 2 km to reach the Southern Barrens, a treeless landscape of rolling valleys and soft bogs inhabited by sheep and caribou. From St. Bride's 4 km is a one-lane paved road to the right leading to Cape St. Mary's— a must see. This side road shifts along the southern portion of the peninsula and the Green Hills for 13 km, until you come to the trailhead and lighthouse.

But fisherfolk aren't the only beings living off the abundant sea life. By walking fifteen minutes along the rocky footpath you come to a massive sea stack separated from the headland by only a 5-meter span, but between you and the rock is a 150-meter drop into the sea. This stack is a nesting area for 50,000 gannet, 10,000 pair of murre, and countless kittiwakes. Birds fly and squawk overhead and around the cliff sides in an unbelievable display of overcrowding. Each pair of gannets uses a rocky outcropping to build their nest and raise their young. When the birds aren't jostling and fighting for extra space, they're leaving for days to dive into the ocean and pick up caplin. You could spend hours watching and delighting in the cacophony and determined

A visitor examines a sea stack covered by thousands of gannets at Cape St. Mary's.

flights of thousands of gannets as they shuttle between the feeding grounds and home.

As you return along Cape St. Mary's Road and **continue** on **100** along Barren Plains, follow the long lonely line of telephone poles. You come to a junction to Point Lance after 9.5 km, and 4.5 km farther you glide down into the town of **Branch**. At one time, Branch was a relatively bustling community, centered on the fish-packing plant, but like so many other fishing crews that once relied on the groundfish industry, the dejected inhabitants wonder where their future lies.

From Branch another long lonely stretch of road follows. **Highway 92**, as it now becomes, is not as hilly or as scenic as 100. The road stumbles along a ridge away from the sea. To your left are extensive barrens and bogs, ideal habitat for caribou, while to your right are the flanks of hills, separating you from the ocean. The barrens slowly surrender to small stands of woods. Small streams skip over the stratified rocks as 92 trudges over a series of long gradual hills. After 42 km of some of the loneliest riding in Atlantic Canada, you arrive at **North Harbour**, complete with a grocery store. The road from this town snuggles up to the arm of water as it climbs gently. Past the village 11 km you come to **91**, climbing to another small section of barrens and Collins Pond. To your left, over a dirt road, is **Cataracts Provincial Park**, 3.5 km from the junction. The two falls that make up the park intersect at the picnic area. The park maintains a series of staircases and boardwalks from which you can admire the views. Back at the intersection with 91 and 92, turn **right**. After 3.7 km, cross the short section of barrens and Rocky River, arriving at **Colinet** and the intersection with 93.

Colinet has no formal accommodations. If you want to stay in town, ask for permission to camp at the community center or school. Everyone is accommodating and friendly, and you can obtain water and provisions at the town's general store.

Colinet to Holyrood Pond Provincial Park: 70.2 kilometers

From Colinet head **south** on **93**, crossing over a small rise. The road, covering 11.3 km, touches Harricott Bay and begins another climb over to **Mount Carmel**, resting on the shore of Salmonier Arm. Mercifully, the road follows the long bay, passing by seaside cottages and culminating at **St. Catherine's**, 6.5 km farther. At the STOP sign turn **right** and a km later turn **right** again, finally riding on **90**. The road follows the opposite shore of Salmonier Arm. You pass **New Bridge** (convenience store), and 10 km from the previous intersection you come to the junction to **St. Joseph's** to the right.

Stock up on supplies at St. Joseph's. From the intersection the road begins to rise again to cross another barren. The undulating and wet terrain is perfect habitat for moose, so keep your eyes open. The road gradually begins dropping through the concave Riverhead Valley, eventually arriving at **Riverhead** after about 19.5 km.

As you pass though the stretched town, you see the battle between the villagers and the economy. A group of women has set up a small crafts co-op and training center to learn the basics of marketing and operating a small business. Some islanders have started to realize the fishing industry's future looks disheartening, so with the help of federally sponsored training programs, they hope to earn a living independent of the fishery. From Riverhead the road climbs a couple of times, staying within view of St. Mary's Harbour. Within 5 km, St. Mary's development begins. The large gas station/grocery store at the town's entrance offers the best selection of food in the area, so stock up for the rest of the day here. Along the road, the villagers have built their bright houses among the glens and lowlands of the headland. The town's position offers a windbreak from any direction. Keep on the lookout for the junction to **La Haye Point Provincial Park**, 9 km from Riverhead. The 2-km road ends at a lighthouse commanding a great view over Gaskiers Bay and the headlands farther north. Back on **90** the road skips along over some small hills and past the warm red, yellow, and blue houses braced against the winds and seas. **St. Mary's**, **Point La Haye**, and **Gaskiers** connect as a series of unbroken villages. If you don't want to camp at Holyrood Pond Provincial Park, Gaskiers provides a bed and breakfast 5.5 km from Point La Haye junction. From Gaskiers the road climbs onto yet another headland until you reach the park 2.8 km farther.

Holyrood Pond Provincial Park to Chance Cove Provincial Park: 79.3 kilometers

From the campground, it's 5.7 km to **St. Vincent's**, another small port just before the causeway separating Holyrood Bay from Holyrood Pond. On the other side of the causeway, now **highway 10**, and 6.4 km farther, you pass **St. Stephens** (stock up here). From this village you begin the tour's longest climb over St. Shotts Country. Over these windy barrens, migrating caribou are so numerous they sometimes stop traffic for up to an hour on "Caribou Road." Although the caribou usually wander through the barrens in splinter herds, just before hunting season starts the Department of Natural Resources herds them and the moose by helicopter to the Avalon Wilderness Area.

The road cruises along the top of the barrens, and, if the winds are with you, you can be almost flying. My companion and I were reaching speeds of up to 60 kilometers per hour, casually pedaling as the wind hurried us to Trepassey. I could only pity the cyclists who were pedaling in the opposite direction across this desolate land. The road passes a barren landscape of ponds, scrub grass, and rocks. As you travel across the barrens, the landscape transforms. The land becomes drier and more stark as boulders and sand begin to dominate. Get ready for the scintillating drop down to Trepassey Harbour and the quick curve at the bottom. Once you've finished dropping, the road circles the far end of the bay and traces the shores of the northeast and northwest arms, finally coming to the junction with **Trepassey** after 31.5 km.

The town's name offers clues as to its character. Meaning "dead or departed" in French, Trepassey is a good spot to retire in for a night if the wind has exhausted you. The name haunts the wrecks of vessels that once littered the shores and the sailors who perished. Bodies used to routinely wash ashore in a part of the harbor the locals named Purgatory. Every cliff and shore from Cape Race to Cape St. Mary's acts as a headstone for the countless ships that wrecked on its shores over the past four centuries. In the past, authorities never revealed the exact number of ships that went down because they were afraid the high numbers would frighten new immigrants and dissuade supply ships from landing at its ports. Ships were lost and never reported, and the locals would bury more unknown sailors.

Back on the main road, continue on **10**. The road climbs slightly, giving wide views over the harbor. Highway 10 then drops past Biscay Bay's sweep of sand. At **Biscay Bay Bridge**, 6.7 km from the junction, salmon leap out of the water while struggling their way upstream to spawn. If the run is plentiful, salmon jump every few seconds and fishers line the bank trying to capture the silver bounty. Along 10, the road follows the shore of Biscay Bay and Portugal Cove until about 4.5 km, where you come to a junction marked by a burnt-out gas station. The road to the right leads to **Mistaken Point Ecological Reserve**.

Mistaken Point holds the only deep-water marine fossils of the Cambrian geological era. Normally, the weight of sediment and rock crushes most soft-celled animals and they never remain as fossils. But at Mistaken Point a fine volcanic ash settled over the creatures, impressing their images before they decayed. The site contains twenty different animals that lived in deep water, including the distant cousins of jellyfish and anemones. The United Nations is considering this strip of coastline, 5 km long and 650 meters wide, as a World Heritage Site.

From the junction to Mistaken Point, continue **left** on **10**. The road begins a gradual climb over more barrens, accentuated by the rolling hills and the small slice of canyon cut by the Portugal River. If you still haven't seen caribou, you have another chance over this section of barrens. As you cross the barrens' summit, marked by the communications towers to your left, you enter an area reduced to wide-open sky, small ponds, and monumental boulders. And right in the center of this primordial land is **Chance Cove Provincial Park** and campground. Another 19 km from the junction to Mistaken Point, turn **right** toward the primitive campground, 5.5 km toward the sea.

Chance Cove Provincial Park to La Manche Provincial Park: 63.1 kilometers

From the junction of **10** and Chance Cove Provincial Park continue northward. As the road intermittently descends, you pass what locals refer to as ponds, which could be anything from a boggy area to a large lake. To your left, in the distance, is the rugged Avalon Wilderness Area. This reserve protects wildlife and attracts hikers, canoeists, and campers. Before visiting the area, travelers must obtain permission

A group of militia soldiers parade the Union Jack flag and their mascot, the Newfoundland dog.

from the Department of Natural Resources in St. John's. After 13 km, you drop to sea level again at **Cappahayden**. Now the wide-open Atlantic rolls into the blunted points of land. From town, the road swings inland over Renews Head and slips beside **Renews Harbour**. Small houses line the road as they face the murky harbor. Across the water the main settlement lies off the main road. Crossing inland, over more hilly terrain, the road skims the village of **Fermeuse** and **Aquaforte**. The road along this section is stunning as it climbs over the bay. The steep walls of the bay shelter the deep harbor, and small houses cling to the island below you. Past Cappahayden 28 km you arrive at **Ferryland**, a small town protected by a long breakwater.

Ferryland maintains full provisions including a Royal Canadian Mounted Police station, a fine bed and breakfast, a restaurant, and a general store. More interesting, though, is Memorial University's ongoing archaeological dig. A small map available at the museum details a short walking tour so you can visit the digs and the laboratory where the students meticulously scrape away centuries of debris from the artifacts.

The road continues, climbing and dropping over headlands for 10 km, to **Cape Broyle**. About 11.5 km farther you arrive at **La Manche Valley Provincial Park**.

The park is worth exploring for its wildlife and scenery. Naturalists have identified moose, beaver, hare, shrew, and fifty species of birds. The first trail in the park, 1 km long, takes you to a waterfall above La

Manche Pond. The second trail of the same length leads to the abandoned town of La Manche, devastated by a storm in 1966.

La Manche Valley Provincial Park to Gushue's Pond Provincial Park: 51.7 kilometers

Continuing, the road from the park skirts the ponds and rivers of the
area. Passing **Tors Cove** after 11 km, and then cycling another hilly
4 km, you arrive at **Mobile**, which has a convenience store. Leaving
Mobile and crossing over Frog Marsh, you drop into the village of **Witless Bay**. Although the town holds little interest, it is the only port on
this tour from where you can take a tour to Witless Bay Seabird Sanctuary. The sanctuary holds one of the most important seabird
colonies in North America. Every summer, the worlds' largest population of petrels, razorbills, kittiwakes, murres, and puffins nests on
the four islands.

From Witless Bay, **10** scales a searing climb, and 3 km farther,
you come to **Witless Bay Line (Highway 13)**. The road leaves the
Atlantic shore, and after 21 km passes more bogs, ponds, and barrens
until you arrive at **Trans-Canada Highway 1**. Turn **left**. For the next
9 km, the double-lane highway weaves between hills and ponds until
you come to the junction to **90**. This road heads back to St. Catherine's,
25 km farther south. **Gushue's Pond Provincial Park**, 9 km farther,
beckons.

Gushue's Pond Provincial Park to Argentia: 68.6 kilometers

Traffic on weekends along this road can be busy, but you have to travel
only 24 km farther over rolling terrain to come to the junction with
Highway 100. Turn **left**. The highway stays high on the barrens until
you pass **Fitzgerald's Pond Provincial Park**. Then the road begins
its long, gradual descent down to Northeast Arm. After riding about
34 km, you arrive at **Dunville**, a small settlement with a motel. From
Dunville the road rises on a ridge overlooking the arm and slips
between one last mound of hills. Past Dunville 7 km you pass the junction for 100 and continue on the Argentia road, arriving back at the
ferry terminal 3.5 km farther. On the way back to the mainland or on
the ferry home, you can't help reflecting on the terrain, the people, and
the wildlife of the land molded by the hand of God.

TOUR NO. 21

BACCALIEU TOUR

Start / Finish: Gushue's Pond Provincial Park/
Gushue's Pond Provincial Park
Distance: 236.6 kilometers (144.3 miles)
Estimated time: 3 days
Terrain: Hilly
Map: Newfoundland and Labrador Official
Highway Map
Connecting tours: Tour No. 20
Connections: Trans-Canada Highway 1

This tour exudes romance. When you pedal through the town of Harbour Grace, you may think of the British naval veteran who became a pirate, plundered the Atlantic Coast, and retired the richest man in the world. When you pass Heart's Content, you admire a man's thirteen-year dream and his unquenchable effort to connect North America and Europe. When you visit the whaling museum in South Dildo, you relive the stories of whalers who risked their lives to light the world. As you travel along the shores of Trinity and Conception bays, you expect a brigantine schooner to sail over the horizon, lilting to the tune of "Jack Was Every Inch a Sailor." It's a land where men had to risk their lives to feed their families.

The terrain greets you as it rolls over the headlands and dips into the inhabited coves. The steeper land lies next to Conception Bay, while you're more likely to meet headwinds on the Trinity Bay side. Usually, winds blowing from the west and southwest cleanse the shore of fog. Either way, provisions are easy to find and the people are more than willing to stop and have a chat. Traffic is moderate along the Trans-Canada Highway, and some heavy traffic flows between Clarke's Beach and Carbonear. So head out onto the Baccalieu Trail and enjoy some of the most striking scenery and friendliest people in Newfoundland. "Long may your big jib draw."

Gushue's Pond Provincial Park to Northern Bay Sands Provincial Park: 91.8 kilometers

From **Gushue's Pond Provincial Park** on **Trans-Canada Highway 1**, head **west**, away from St. John's. Shortly, after 3 km, you arrive at the interchange for **70**. Head **right** along the interchange and up 70. This highway, already high, climbs and dips over Nine Island Ridge for 14 km until you pass the intersection for 60. Continue straight on **70**, and 3

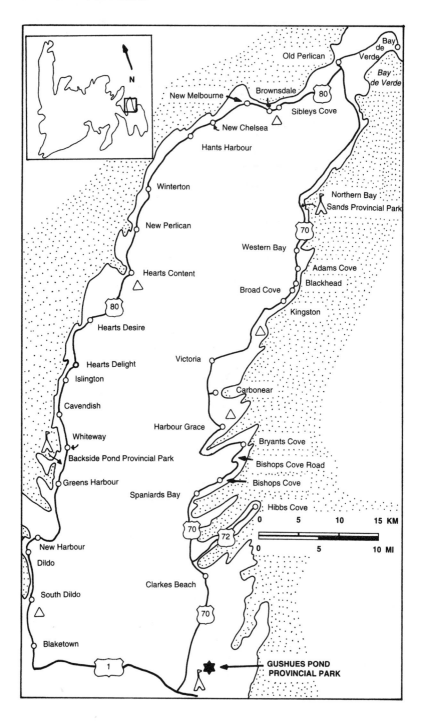

km farther you come to **Clarke's Beach**, nestled at the head of Bay de Grave. The following section is the most populated area outside St. John's, so expect moderate traffic.

Past the grocery store 400 meters is the optional, one-way excursion along 72, ending at Hibbs Cove. This small settlement is everything you could imagine a Newfoundland port to be. Square houses sit on the shore of a harbor encircled by large rocks. The Fisherman's Museum displays tools and furniture used by the peninsula's early settlers.

Back along **70**, the traffic increases and the tour's messiest part begins. Strip malls line the road, so be careful of cars making dangerous turns. About 9 km from the 72 junction, just beyond the town of **Spaniard's Bay**, turn **right** on **Bishop's Cove Road**. (If you want to avoid the two grueling hills and some magnificent coastal scenery, continue on 70, climbing over Alderberry Hill to arrive at Riverhead.) The tour follows along a small ridge overlooking Spaniard's Bay, and after 4.5 km of striking scenery you come to the picturesque village of **Bishop's Cove**. The road dips and climbs past homes perched on the rocky peninsula. Horses graze atop cliffs that drop into the greenish-blue water. The road becomes **Main Street** as it skips through town and ends 1.7 km farther. Keep **left** and **left** again, climbing a steep hill up to the cemetery. Stop at the top of the hill and take in the grand sweep of scenery. Bodies of water—Spaniard's Bay, Bay Roberts, and Bay de Grave—search deep into the harbors for granite to carve and wash away. Ports sit on the peninsulas like lustrous jeweled rings. A km from the last corner, after the cemetery, turn **right** on **Bryants Cove Road**. The road rises slightly and then begins a long, ripping drop into **Bryants Cove**. You have stupendous views of the *drook* (steep-sided valley) and Sheppards Hill beyond. You'll be at sea level after 4 km of this glorious downhill. You now face the most painful hill of the tour. Luckily, traffic is light, so you can switch back, reducing the grade. The road drops just as quickly on the hill's other side, and soon you're on the south shore of **Harbour Grace**. The town is across the bay, stretched along the shore. Haunting the bay, the skeletons of trawlers and dories rust in the water and conceal their stories of abandonment. At the harbor's head the silt anchors the bulk of a woeful passenger steamer. The vessel, stained by tears of rust, has been run aground, left for decades, and forsaken. Past Bryants Cove 6 km you arrive at the harbor's head. Turn **right** on **70**. Shortly after passing the *Spirit of Harbour Grace*, an airplane that children climb on, and 700 meters from the last corner, keep **right**, following **Water Street**. The town starts lining the road immediately, and 3.5 km farther you pass a fish-packing plant and the wharf, officially the town's center.

Water, fire, and air characterize Harbour Grace's history. The French first settled the area in 1550 and named it Havre de Grace. It remained a quiet, fishing port until 1610 when Peter Easton built a fort where the Customs House stands today.

For years this pirate/admiral terrorized the east coast. Easton, a veteran of the British navy, gained control of the western North Atlantic with ships manned by fishermen he recruited or pressed into service.

An abandoned, rusting passenger steamer at the head of Harbour Grace Bay

Sailing on the Atlantic winds and using Harbour Grace as his refuge, he plundered coastal villages, looted French and Portuguese fishing boats, and pillaged English vessels. In 1612, embarking from Ferryland, he attacked the Spanish colonies in Puerto Rico. When the gold filled his ships to the gunwales he left for the Mediterranean where the old swashbuckler bought a palace in France, became a marquis, and died as one of the world's richest men.

Harbour Grace grew in the seventeenth century, and it became the province's second largest town. Then, from 1814 to 1944, three disastrous fires leveled most of the town. Only a few stone buildings remained: St. Paul's Anglican Church (1835), the Church of the Immaculate Conception (1889), and one of the oldest jails and courthouses in Canada.

Harbour Grace's importance declined, but its position in the Atlantic made it ideal for daring aviators. In 1931, Wiley Post used the town as a staging area for his successful flight around the world, and in 1932 Amelia Earhart left here to fly across the Atlantic solo. Today, the museum, once the Customs House, details the town's colorful history.

The museum is only 600 meters from the wharf, and 200 meters farther you arrive at the imposing Church of the Immaculate Conception.

From the church, turn **left** up **Cathedral Street**, and after only 100 meters merge with **70**. After another 4 km and a climb over Bristol's Headland, you come to the junction for **Carbonear**. Highway 70 continues, circumventing town and climbing again to allow great views over the town and Carbonear Bay. The road descends to **Victoria**, arriving after 6.5 km. Turn **right**, following **70**, and continue a gentle downhill to the junction for **Salmon Cove Sands Provincial Park**, 5.5 km farther. The park, 2 km from the road, is only three-quarters paved and ends at a gorgeous cove surrounded by black cliffs, pink sand, and jagged rocks thrusting out of the bay. Back on 70, the road passes Salmon Cove Pond and curves up to a wild, rocky area. After you pass the small section of barrens you come to a remarkable section of coastal riding. Here, the road hugs the cliff's ledge, eventually arriving at Kingston, 8.5 km from Salmon Cove. The next section of road crosses a string of settlements that dot the coast like icing flowers on a birthday cake.

The terrain becomes less steep. The hills now rise gradually from the water and crawl to the wild uplands. Each of the villages has a grocery store to keep you supplied with provisions before Northern Bay. As you roll over this area you pass the villages of **Kingston**, **Broad Cove**, **Blackhead**, **Adams Cove**, and **Western Bay**.

Western Bay, 7 km from Kingston, is the birthplace of E. J. Pratt, one of Canada's greatest poets. Growing up on the wild coast, his poetry spoke of Newfoundlanders' struggles with nature; he portrayed the anonymous hero and the heroic act. He wrote epics of the building of the Trans-Canada railway, the persecution of Franciscans, and common heroes who risked their lives in small, open boats.

From Western Bay the road flanks the ocean until you arrive at **Northern Bay Sands Provincial Park**, 7 km farther.

Northern Bay Sands Provincial Park to Backside Pond Provincial Park: 94.7 kilometers

From the park, continue up **70**. After another 11 km of rolling terrain you pass by a lookout over the Bay de Verde Peninsula. The peninsula grasps the water like a giant talon plunging for prey. You continue to wind past bogs and transitional barrens for 7 km until you come to the junction for Old Perlican and the Bay de Verde Peninsula.

To reach the peninsula, you take a side trip on the continuation of 70. After 5 km, the road leads to the village of **Bay de Verde**. This large fishing community's harbor was created when a hill of rock was blasted into the harbor to form the breakwater. Offshore is Baccalieu Island, a nesting site for gannets, petrels, and puffins.

Back at the junction, the town of **Old Perlican** lies ahead of you. Turn **left** on **80**, tracing the peninsula's northern edge. Along 80 the terrain calms down, and the road rolls lightly over minor hills. Over the next 24 km you pass **Sibleys Cove**, holding the small Sparks Heritage House. The house, restored to its original condition, contains artifacts from the Sparks family, early pioneers in the area. You also pass the settlements of **Brownsdale**, **New Melbourne**, and **New Chelsea**. Between New Melbourne and New Chelsea you have to climb over Gaze Hill, more than 100 meters high. After 24 km, you reach the turn for **Hant's Harbour**. This small town, 300 meters from the main road, nestled in the harbor and protected by Wester Head and lighthouse-capped Custer Head, also has a small unofficial museum. Mr. Sam Loder, living across from the town hall, has collected tools, furniture, guns, and memorabilia for decades. He's happy to show visitors his collection and always has a story to tell. From Hant's Harbour Road, 80 becomes more hilly. You'll find this side of the peninsula is more forested; the hills rise and fall between the coves and ponds. You pass **Winterton** and arrive at **New Perlican**, 16 km from Hant's Harbour. As you cycle along the windward side of the bay, you see houses scattered on the leeward side of the bay, the red and white spiral-painted lighthouse, and, through the mouth of the bay, the mainland across Trinity Bay. Ride 5 km from New Perlican to arrive at **Heart's Content Cable Station**—terminus of one of the most tenacious projects of the 1800s.

When you visit the center, you become overwhelmed by the machinery and engineering chicanery used to send Morse code signals across the ocean. Rooms of switches, mysterious boxes of wires and buttons, and an insulated vault are testaments to years of ingenuity, perseverance, and ambition.

Just 200 meters down 80 you come to Jack's Grocery Store, an icon of community spirit and old-time friendliness. This working shop feels like a living museum where you breathe the atmosphere of a dry-goods shop as it was decades ago. From Jack's, it is 700 meters to the junction to 74, heading back to Victoria. Turn **right**, following **80**. From Heart's Content 9 km, the road twists past small hills and Seal Cove Pond and you pass **Heart's Desire**, which has a grocery and a freshwater swimming hole. Beyond the town, the road becomes flatter and follows Trinity Bay's shore. After another 6 km, you arrive at **Heart's Delight**. The road swoops past **Islington**, and 7.5 km from Heart's Desire you arrive at **Cavendish** (grocery). The road continues to follow the bays, and 3.5 km farther, you arrive at **Whiteway** (grocery). About 4 km from Whiteway you come to **Backside Pond Provincial Park**.

Backside Pond Provincial Park to Gushue's Pond Provincial Park: 50.1 kilometers

Continuing on 80, shortly after leaving the park you pass **Green's Harbour**, **New Harbour**, and the settlement of **Dildo**. These towns sit off the main road, so they're hard to find. After 21.5 km with only one substantial hill and a long coastal road along Dildo Arm, you come to **South Dildo**—remarkable for its sealing and whaling museum. You can't miss it thanks to the huge whale sculpture leaping out of the ground beside the museum. When you visit the museum expect to see artifacts documenting the importance whaling and sealing had on the Trinity shore. Exhibits highlight the traditions, songs, and legends of

A bike parked next to the skull of a blue whale in front of the whaling museum at South Dildo

great whalers such as Highliner George and Captain Mahle. From South Dildo the road climbs slightly out of Dildo Arm and Trinity Bay. It now passes Dildo Pond and **Blaketown**. Just beyond Blaketown, notice the mink farms to the left.

Almost 8 km from South Dildo you arrive at the **Trans-Canada Highway**. Turn **left**. The road rises over ridges and drops past ponds for a deserted 21 km back to **Gushue's Pond Provincial Park**.

APPENDIX 1

WHAT TO TAKE

Clothing

1 pair shoes
2 pairs socks
1 pair pants
2 pairs cycling shorts
2 pairs underwear
1 T-shirt
1 pair arm warmers
1 cycling jacket
1 pair tights (optional)

1 pair swimming shorts
1 hat
1 pair walking shorts
    (optional)
1 bandana
1 pair cycling gloves
1 pair sandals (optional)
1 watch with alarm
rain jacket

Bicycle

1 bike
1 helmet
1 odometer
2 oversized water bottles

2 bungee cords
1 lock
2 sets of panniers
1 mirror

Bike Parts and Tools

1 brake cable (long)
1 derailleur cable (long)
1 chain breaker
spare wire for emergency repairs
1 spare tube
1 pump
3 spokes for both rear and
    front wheels (optional)

spoke key (optional)
tire levers
adjustable wrench
freewheel remover (optional)
crank remover (optional)
chain oil
patch kit

Camping Equipment

sleeping bag (optional)
sleeping pad (optional)
tent (optional)
stove (optional)
spoon

stove (optional)
lighter
flashlight
utility knife
pots (optional)

First-Aid Kit

tensor bandage
alcohol pads
pain relievers
heat rub
gauze pads (small and large)

bandages
adhesive tape
sunscreen
lip balm
anti-bacterial cream

Personal Needs

brush and/or comb
soap
shampoo
razor and blades
toothbrush and toothpaste

sunglasses
eyeshades
towel
earplugs

Documents

travelers checks (optional)
bank card
credit card

address list
personal identification
waist pouch

Miscellaneous

personal stereo (optional)
daypack
pen and paper
ziplock bags
journal

travel guide
maps
camera (optional)
binoculars (optional)
compass

APPENDIX 2

METRIC CONVERSION

Temperatures

To convert °C to °F multiply by 1.8 and add 32.
To convert °F to °C subtract 32 and multiply by ⅝.

Distance

A kilometer is approximately 0.6 mile. To convert kilometers into miles multiply by 0.6.

1 inch = 2.54 centimeters	1 centimeter = 0.39 inch
1 foot = 30.48 centimeters	1 meter = 3.28 feet
1 yard = 0.91 meter	1 meter = 1.09 yards
1 mile = 1.61 kilometers	1 kilometer = 0.62 mile

Volume

1 U.S. gallon = 3.79 liters
1 U.S. quart = 0.95 liter
6 U.S. gallons = 5 imperial gallons
The imperial measure is 20 percent larger than the U.S. measure.

Weight

ounces to grams, multiply by 28.35
grams to ounces, multiply by 0.035
pounds to kilograms, multiply by 0.45
kilograms to pounds, multiply by 2.2046
U.S. tons to kilograms, multiply by 907

APPENDIX 3

TEMPERATURES CHART

From the records of the Canadian Government Travel Bureau

High/Low Temperatures in °C

	Jan.	Feb.	Mar.	April	May	June	July	Aug.	Sept.	Oct.	Nov.	Dec.
Saint John *New Brunswick*	-2/-11	-2/-11	3/-6	8/0	14/5	18/9	21/12	21/13	18/10	13/5	7/-1	0/-8
Halifax *Nova Scotia*	0/-8	-1/-9	3/-4	8/0	15/5	20/10	24/13	23/14	20/11	14/6	8/1	2/-5
Charlottetown *Prince Edward Island*	-3/-12	-4/-12	1/-7	7/-1	14/4	20/10	24/15	24/15	19/11	13/6	6/0	-1/-7
St. John's *Newfoundland*	1/-6	0/-7	1/-5	6/-2	10/2	15/6	21/11	20/12	16/7	11/3	7/0	2/-5

APPENDIX 4

ACCOMMODATIONS

This appendix can help if you decide to deviate from a tour's itinerary. For each tour I've listed the towns and the types of accommodations each provides as you would pass them during the tour. Make sure you reserve a space during July and August.

    B&B = Bed and Breakfast
      C = Cottage
   CG = Campground
      I = Inn
     H = Hotel
    M = Motel
    R = Resort
   YH = Youth Hostel

Tour No. 1

Accommodations: Halifax (B&B, YH, H), Prospect (B&B), West Dover (B&B), Hacketts Cove (B&B), Peggys Cove (B&B), Glen Margaret (CG), Indian Harbour (M, C, CG).

Tour No. 2

Accommodations: Boutiliers Point (M), Black Point (M), Hubbards (M, CG), Deep Cove (H), Graves Island (CG), East Chester (B&B), Chester (M, B&B), Gold River (B&B), Western Shore (H), Indian Point (B&B), Martins River (CG), Mahone Bay (B&B), Lunenburg (H, B&B, CG), Bayport (CG), Riverport (B&B, CG), East LaHave (B&B, CG), Petite Rivière (B&B), Rissers Beach Provincial Park (CG), Broad Cove (B&B), Brooklyn (M), Liverpool (B&B, H).

Tour No. 3

Accommodations: Yarmouth (B&B, H, CG), Darling Lake (H, YH, CG), Meteghan (B&B), Meteghan River (H), Saulnierville (B&B), Church Point (B&B, CG), Weymouth (H), Digby (H, B&B, CG), Annapolis Royal (H, B&B, CG), South Milford (H), Maitland Bridge (CG), Caledonia (H), Hibernia (CG), Liverpool (B&B, H), White Point (H), Summerville Beach (B&B), Hunts Point (H), Port Mouton (B&B, H), Sable River (B&B, CG), Lockeport (B&B, CG), Shelburne (B&B, H, CG), Clarks Harbour (B&B), Barrington (CG), Barrington Passage (H), Woods Harbour (B&B), Tusket (B&B).

Tour No. 4

Accommodations: Annapolis Royal (B&B, I/M, CG), Granville Ferry (B&B), Port Royal (B&B), Delaps Cove (B&B, CG), Bridgetown (I, B&B), Valleyview Provincial Park (CG), Paradise (B&B), Lawrencetown (B&B), Middleton (I, M, B&B, CG), Wilmot (H, CG), Kingston (H, CG), Auburn (B&B), Aylesford (CG), Grafton (CG), Berwick (I, B&B, M), Kentville (H, B&B, CG), Wolfville (B&B, I), Grand Pré (M, B&B, I, CG), Windsor (I, M, B&B, CG).

Tour No. 5

Accommodations: Amherst (B&B, H/M, CG), Nappan (B&B, M, CG), Advocate Harbour (CG), Spencers Island (B&B), Port Greville (B&B), Springhill (M), Parrsboro (B&B, M, I, CG), Wallace (B&B, I, CG), Pugwash (B&B), Oxford (B&B, M), Port Howe (I), Lorneville (I, B&B, CG).

Tour No. 6

Accommodations: Antigonish (H, B&B, CG), Cribbons Point (B&B).

Tour No. 7

Accommodations: Baddeck (H/M, B&B, CG), Nyanza (M), North East Margaree (H, C, CG), Margaree Forks (M, H), Margaree Harbour (H/M, I, R), Chéticamp (M, H, CG), Pleasant Bay (M, CG), Cape North (H, B&B, CG), Dingwall (H), White Point (B&B), Ingonish (H, CG), Ingonish Centre (H, R), Ingonish Beach (H, I, R, CG), Breton Cove (B&B), Indian Brook (B&B, CG), Tarbotvale (B&B), South Gut, St. Anns (M).

Tour No. 8

Accommodations: Sydney (M, H, B&B), Marion Bridge (B&B, CG), Hillside (CG), Albert Bridge (B&B, CG), Louisbourg (B&B, CG)), Glace Bay (B&B).

Tour No. 9

Accommodations: St. John (H/M, I, B&B, CG), Chance Harbour (B&B), Lepreau (CG), New River Beach Provincial Park (CG), Pocologan (H, B&B, CG), Blacks Harbour (B&B), North Head (H, I, B&B), Castalia (C), White Cove (B&B), Grand Harbour (C), Anchorage Provincial Park (CG), Seal Cove (C, B&B), St. George (B&B, H, CG), St. Andrews (H, B&B, I, C, CG), Oak Point Provincial Park (CG), St. Stephen (M, B&B, C, CG).

Tour No. 10

Accommodations: St. John (H/M, I, B&B, CG), Westfield Ferry Landing (CG), Crystal Beach (CG), Kingston (C), Hampton (B&B, I), Cambridge Narrows (B&B, CG), Jemseg (H), Gagetown (B&B, I), Hampstead (B&B), Evandale (H), Oak Point (CG).

Tour No. 11

Accommodations: Fredericton (H, B&B, YH), Mactaquac (CG), Woolastook Provincial Park (CG), Dumfries (H), Hawkshaw (CG), Nackawic (H, C, B&B, CG), Woodstock (H, B&B, CG), Hampton (I, B&B), Florenceville (H, CG), Muniac Provincial Park (CG), Perth-Andover (H, B&B, CG), Plaster Rock (H, C, CG), New Denmark (B&B), Grand Falls (H, C, B&B, CG).

Tour No. 12

Accommodations: Chatham (H, I, C, CG), Loggieville (CG), Bay Du Vin (B&B), Pointe-Sapin (CG), Kouchibouguac National Park (CG), Saint-Louis-De-Kent (H, CG), Richibucto (H, B&B, C, CG), Rexton (C), Saint-Edouard-de-Kent (C, CG), Bouctouche (H, B&B, C, CG), Cocagne (H), Shediac Bridge (H), Shediac (H, B&B, I, C, CG).

Tour No. 13

Accommodations: Jacques Cartier Provincial Park (CG), Alberton (I, B&B), Fortune Cove (C), Mill River Provincial Park (CG), O'Leary (B&B), Cedar Dunes Provincial Park (CG), West Point (B&B, I), West Cape (C), Burton (C), Waterford (CG, C), Skinners Pond (C), Anglo Tignish (B&B), Tignish (B&B, C).

Tour No. 14

Accommodations: Miscouche (C), Abram-Village (C), Maximeville (C, B&B), Cape-Egmont (C), Mont Carmel (B&B).

Tour No. 15

Accommodations: Victoria (I, H).

Tour No. 16

Accommodations: Cavendish (CG, M, C, B&B), South Rustico (CG), North Rustico (M), South Rustico (I), Brackley Beach (CG, H, B&B), Rustico Island (CG), Stanhope Beach (CG, B&B), Stanhope (C), Dalvay-by-the-Sea Hotel (H), Covehead (CG), Oyster Bed Bridge (CG), New Glasgow (C).

Tour No. 17

Accommodations: Strathgartney Provincial Park (CG), Bonshaw (I, B&B), Cumberland (C), Fairview (CG, C), Churchill (CG, B&B).

Tour No. 18

Accommodations: Red Point Provincial Park (C, CG), Souris (I, M), Campbells Cove (CG), North Lake (C, M).

Tour No. 19

Accommodations: Lord Selkirk Provincial Park (CG), Gladstone (CG), Murray Harbour (CG, C), Panmure Island Provincial Park (CG), Northumberland Provincial Park (CG), Eldon (H, M), Lower Montague (M), Montague (H, I, B&B), Wood Islands (M), Panmure Island (B&B), Pinette (C), Orwell (B&B).

Tour No. 20

Accommodations: Freshwater (B&B), Placentia (H), St. Bride's (I, R), Branch (B&B), Gaskiers (B&B), Holyrood Pond Provincial Park (CG), Trepassey (B&B), Chance Cove Provincial Park (CG), Cappahayden (C), Aquaforte (C), Ferryland (I), La Manche Valley Provincial Park (CG), Tors Cove (C), Witless Bay (B&B), Gushue's Pond Provincial Park (CG), Whitbourne Junction (M), Fitzgerald's Pond Provincial Park (CG).

Tour No. 21

Accommodations: Bay Roberts (M, B&B), Blaketown (CG), Carbonear (M, B&B, CG), Clarke's Beach (CG), Dildo (CG), Harbour Grace (M, B&B, CG), Heart's Content (M), Heart's Delight (B&B, CG), New Perlican (CG), Northern Bay Sands Provincial Park (M, CG), Salmon Cove (CG), Spaniard's Bay (M), Victoria (CG), Western Bay (CG), Whitbourne (M), Whiteway (CG), Winterton (M, CG), Backside Pond Provincial Park (CG), Gushue's Pond Provincial Park (CG).

APPENDIX 5

PROVINCIAL TOURISM

Nova Scotia Travel Information, Corporatel, Suite 501, 2695 Dutch Village Road, Halifax, Nova Scotia, Canada B3L 4V2, 1-800-565-0000

New Brunswick Tourist Information, PO Box 12345, Fredericton, New Brunswick, Canada E3B 5C3, 1-800-561-0123

Prince Edward Island, PO Box 940E, Charlottetown, Prince Edward Island, Canada C1A 7M5, 1-800-565-0267

Newfoundland Department of Development, PO Box 8730, St. John's, Newfoundland, Canada A1B 4K2, 1-800-563-6353

INDEX

ABOUT THE AUTHOR

Walter's cycling experiences began as a young lad, when he crashed his brother's oversized bike into a barrel of used grease outside of a fast-food chicken restaurant. Since then, his bicycling adventures have taken him through over 25 countries and every province and territory in Canada. His first book, *Latin America by Bike,* was researched during a two-year journey through that part of the world. Currently, he works in Toronto, Canada as a commercial photographer and travel writer, far away from chicken fat.

THE MOUNTAINEERS, founded in 1906, is a nonprofit outdoor activity and conservation club, whose mission is "to explore, study, preserve, and enjoy the natural beauty of the outdoors. . . ." Based in Seattle, Washington, the club is now the third-largest such organization in the United States, with 15,000 members and four branches throughout Washington State.

The Mountaineers sponsors both classes and year-round outdoor activities in the Pacific Northwest, which include hiking, mountain climbing, ski-touring, snowshoeing, bicycling, camping, kayaking and canoeing, nature study, sailing, and adventure travel. The club's conservation division supports environmental causes through educational activities, sponsoring legislation, and presenting informational programs. All club activities are led by skilled, experienced volunteers, who are dedicated to promoting safe and responsible enjoyment and preservation of the outdoors.

The Mountaineers Books, an active, nonprofit publishing program of the club, produces guidebooks, instructional texts, historical works, natural history guides, and works on environmental conservation. All books produced by The Mountaineers are aimed at fulfilling the club's mission.

If you would like to participate in these organized outdoor activities or the club's programs, consider a membership in The Mountaineers. For information and an application, write or call The Mountaineers, Club Headquarters, 300 Third Avenue West, Seattle, Washington 98119; (206) 284-6310.

Send or call for our catalog of more than 300 outdoor titles:

 The Mountaineers Books
1001 SW Klickitat Way, Suite 201
Seattle, WA 98134
1-800-553-4453